SOUL SELFISH

SOUL
SELFISH

THE AWAKENING OF A
"GOOD GIRL"

JANE WYKER

SOUL SELFISH
The Awakening of a "Good Girl"

ISBN   978-1-61961-418-5   *Hardcover*
       978-1-61961-426-0   *Ebook*

LIONCREST
PUBLISHING

To my many inspiring
teachers who have
led me to my soul.

ACKNOWLEDGMENTS

I AM PROUD TO SAY THIS IS MY FIRST BOOK, WHICH I STARTED writing at age 78. It has become a reality out of the loving and generous support of so many—some that are part of my active life and others who have passed and are not aware of their immense contribution to it.

My deep gratitude goes to:

The many authors who wrote courageous books about the inner life that I devoured. Thank you for your brilliance that opened me to myself.

Barbara Stanny, my mentor and friend, who insisted that either I clean up my resistance or I would never write. Her laser-like clarity sliced through my excuses, allowing me to begin one of the great joys of my life. Barbara, you are the mother of this book.

My husband Bob, who after reading my first few stories, continually supported my writing. He became my preliminary editor, encouraging me with his enthusiasm, asking countless questions and making suggestions. Most importantly, loving me through it all.

Lara Wisniewski, my first editor. She was the teacher I needed from the start. More than that: my psychological and spiritual confidante, literary advisor and writing coach, covering the basic elements of writing and pointing out the deepest internal gaps in my stories.

Ann Maynard, my final editor who challenged me to "up my game" and, with a sharp knife, insightfully cut through that which didn't belong while greatly enhancing that which did.

My publishers, Lioncrest who made the process of producing this book a delight. And to my creative marketing team, Shelton Interactive who teach me about websites and social media, coaxing me into the world in a brand new, exciting way.

My family of origin: my parents, brother and my second mother, Aunt Rose. The family I created, my first husband, four children and their families for all the lessons, the joys and sorrows, the wide breath of experiences that were fertile ground for me to become who I am. Thank you for the roles of daughter, sister, niece, wife, mother and grandmother, the many faces of a woman.

Thank you to my precious friends with whom I played, laughed, leaned on and supported, and still do.

Thank you to the Universe that blesses me daily.

CONTENTS

introduction

"GOOD GIRL"

IN 1960 MY HUSBAND WERNER CAME HOME FROM WORK, thrilled to tell me that he had arranged for season tickets to New York Giants football games at Yankee Stadium. He was excited about how special this was since there was no open admission seating to the games, and tickets were hard to come by for even a single game. Although I wasn't enthusiastic about football, I was willing to give it a try.

Our tickets were located in the end zone of the upper deck. The first time we arrived at our seats I was disturbed to see a supporting pillar partially blocking my view down the length of the field. As I sank into my seat, I glanced over to see if my husband was similarly frustrated. Werner had a clear view. I didn't say anything since, after all, this was much more important to him. He didn't say a word about the pole either.

Week after week from September through December, the same loyal fans showed up with anticipation and passion in rain or shine, mild or freezing temperatures. It was an established community, a happy camaraderie, always unified with a single purpose: rooting for a Giants victory. Familiar faces were always sitting in the same section, rows, and seats. From time to time, I would see a woman with a season "regular," then a different woman a few games later. I would smile and say "hello" and he would too. It was a secret we shared.

The applause was deafening as each Giant was announced and ran onto the field. Cheers from more than sixty thousand people echoed through the stadium when great plays were made, just as a chorus of groans poured over the stands when hopes were dashed. An outstanding pass, run, or defensive play electrified the crowd, changing the game and the collective mood in a split second. There was hearty laughter during halftime as fans threw dozens of colorful beach balls around the stadium, but nothing was as exciting as a moment of greatness when we all celebrated together.

With each home game I became more interested. It was fun to be at the stadium. The excitement was palpable. A deep stillness in the huge crowd would spontaneously burst into wild cheers at any moment. I was becoming more familiar with the players, the rules, and some of the finer points of strategy. I cared about what happened. I was becoming a Giants fan!

Yet, at every game I found myself bobbing from the left of the pole to the right of the pole, and then from the right of the pole to the left of the pole, trying to see what was happening. Sometimes I was frustrated, other times annoyed, unable to see whether a long pass was completed or dropped, or if a fumble was recovered or lost. The loud roars or moans told me what I had missed. Each week, my husband sat in the unobstructed seat and I sat in the obstructed one. Incredibly, this arrangement continued for ten years, with neither of us ever questioning it. I made no request and he made no offer.

Clearly, it wasn't a matter of intelligence. Werner and I were Cornell classmates and graduates. We both knew that one of the seats was highly preferable. Why didn't I ever say: "Let's take turns?" Why didn't I suggest changing seats from game to game or from half to half? Why didn't he? Why didn't I ever express my irritation at being blocked from seeing the action, often missing exciting, sometimes game-changing plays? Was inequality so deeply entrenched in each of us? In the culture at large? Or both? Why was I willing to accept this?

I cannot speak for Werner, but I can say for myself that asking for an alternate arrangement never entered my mind. It is very embarrassing to admit how little I stood for my own pleasure, a shame I still carry with me. It is an indignity that continues to concern me about my legacy to my three sons and daughter all these years later. What had I modeled for them by that abdication, not to speak of the sadness I have for the many years I did not stand up for myself?

It took me many years, many tears, and a lot of hard work to realize those questions could be answered with a few simple words that were rooted in a complex history: I was a "good girl."

Good girls were quiet. They demanded nothing. They never asked to be put first. They certainly were not selfish. Good girls paid attention to the desires of others, even at their own expense. "Good Girl" was a pattern that threaded through my childhood, adolescence, college, early marriage, and motherhood. I sometimes wrestle with it even today. I wanted to be a good daughter, good wife, and good mother. In doing so, I lost touch with my voice, my dreams, and my truth. I had lost connection with my very soul.

I am now eighty. For forty-six years I have been taking steps to discover more of my genuine self. My focus inward has remained the bedrock of my life, my passion and purpose. I have let go of false beliefs while healing and releasing painful emotions. I have learned to forgive. I realized that barriers I thought existed in the outer world actually lived in me. I now prioritize my desires and pleasure, and I have grown to feel more self-love and happiness. I know that hearing and trusting my soul's whisper, rather than the shrill cry of my ego's incessant demand to be seen and valued, is a lifetime process. I am still learning.

I wrote *Soul Selfish* to contribute to your self-love, creativity, and happiness. I encourage you to look within and release the thoughts and feelings that limit you. Perhaps you might find a more compelling glimpse of the treasures buried in your soul, waiting to be discovered. Perhaps you will connect with your innate talents. Perhaps you will choose forgiveness, letting go of the past. Perhaps you will open your heart to yourself and to more freedom. What blessings these would be! I would be honored to inspire you to focus inward and create your own rewards, both for your happiness and to help create a more compassionate world. My wish is for you to connect with and fulfill the dreams of your soul.

So I ask you: Are you the genuine, gifted, joyful person you were born to be? Is the person you are showing up as a reflection of the true you? Whether you are a man or a woman, you can only share who you think you are. Who are you, dear reader?

o n e

BEGINNINGS

I WAS RAISED IN A TWO-FAMILY HOUSE IN THE FLATBUSH section of Brooklyn until I was thirteen. My grandmother, Baba, lived upstairs with my Aunt Rose and Uncle Abe. I lived downstairs with my parents and my older brother, Walter. Dad did his best to take care of his three children: Mom, Walt, and me.

When Mom's father died, she had insisted on moving back into her family home to share the burden of caring for her mother with her older sister, Rose. She prevailed over Dad's strong objections, a disastrous decision but one that was in accord with her mother's expectations. It was an act of huge devotion, loyalty, and kindness to Aunt Rose. Even as grown women both sisters were controlled by Baba, acceding to her every demand. Baba believed that her daughters were there to serve her, and they spent their lives doing just that. I was born into that household—a family of good girls.

I never heard Baba say a kind word or offer a generous or sweet gesture. I never saw her smile. Even as a grown woman, Mom was as terrified as a child in Baba's presence. She was deeply depressed, cried a lot, and spent most mornings avoiding her mother. I can't imagine what it was like for Mom to have had such a harsh, bitter mother, or what kind of mother Baba must have had.

The neighborhood kids were also afraid of Baba because she often confiscated their balls when they landed in our yard. Once, when she was angry with my brother, she grabbed his baseball bat and threw it into the coal furnace. He was screaming and I was crying as we stood in the basement, watching helplessly and smelling it burn.

Despite having a devoted husband, children and several friends, Mom's life was mostly about coping with Baba. She had trouble sleeping and took phenobarbital pills for many years, routinely prescribed by my Uncle Ben, a physician. She slept late and woke up groggy most mornings. I played with my dolls and toys by myself, waiting for her to get up. Staying home wasn't much fun when Aunt Rose and Daddy were at work and Walt was in school.

Mom rarely took me out, and I had no friends to play with. Sometimes I wished that she would come outside and play dolls with me, or hopscotch, jump rope, "A My Name is Alice," tag, running bases, hide and seek, punch ball, stoopball, catch—play something, *anything*, or at least watch. Instead she listened to her friends' problems, giving them advice on long phone calls while I played alone.

I was excited to start kindergarten so I could go to school like Walt. I was shy when I saw the kids in my class in the schoolyard since I didn't know any of them. A few minutes later a teacher called for all kindergartners to get on line to go inside. I began to cry and clung to Mom. She gently pried me off her leg, telling me she had to leave and I had to go to school. I was scared, having no idea what school would be like. The teacher was nice. She put her hand on my shoulder and told me there were many things to play with upstairs. Her kindness made me feel better.

From that day on, school was my playground. I loved it, every minute of it. I loved being with all the kids, playing games with them, doing art projects, and listening to the teacher read to us. I couldn't wait to go every morning. I found school easy and fun and loved learning. It was so different from home where I felt bored and lonely.

First grade was even better, with new friends and much to learn: reading, writing, and numbers. I was glad that Mom came to my open school morning even though she looked as large as a mountain from the perspective of my small desk. Her obesity always embarrassed me.

I did so well in first grade that I skipped second grade. One evening after dinner Mom asked if I would like to read her a story. It was the first time she ever did that, and I was surprised and excited! I felt special since I was a good reader and proud of it. We lay down together on my bed. I nestled into her with my head resting on her arm as she attentively listened to me read. Feeling comfortable and engrossed in the story, I wasn't even aware that Daddy was removing a splinter from my heel. Suddenly he interrupted my reading to victoriously announce that the splinter was out. Immediately, Mom got up from the bed. I felt hurt that she didn't want to hear me finish the story and tricked by both of them. I became very quiet. Mom complimented Daddy on removing the splinter, and they both complimented me on being a good patient. What I wanted to hear was that I was a good reader. Neither of them ever asked me to read to them again, nor did they ever read to me.

Even though Mom was unhappy, she was gentle with me. She never fostered competition between my brother and me or put pressure on me to perform in school or elsewhere. She also never acknowledged any of my abilities. Nothing I did or accomplished seemed to matter. The most attention I ever received from her was when she complimented me for being undemanding. I interpreted that as encouragement never to ask for anything. With Mom unable to take care of herself, let alone me, it seemed best for me to be good. I was determined not to disturb her or cause trouble as Walt did. Mom hid in fear of her mother, and I hid my loneliness from mine.

Daddy was a lawyer and very proud of it, having gone to Brooklyn Law School at night after his full-time salesman's job. He personified dignity and was always a gentleman, dressed formally in tie and jacket. He was very rational—a starched white shirt guy who was disconnected from his feelings.

He started his law practice at the beginning of the Great Depression. Economic worries weighed him down for decades as he helped to support his parents in addition to our family. Daddy placed a high value on possessions and professional standing, typically living a little beyond his means to appear richer than he was. He always drove expensive cars while shuffling his monthly bills, paying them as he could. He believed that money was the road to happiness, and that education was the means to that end.

Daddy's arrival home from work was a high point of my day. When I was old enough, I often went to the subway station to wait for him so that we could walk home together hand in hand. Skipping, hopping, and singing, I had him all to myself, before he paid attention to Mom's sadness and Walt's misbehavior. He was always delighted to see me waiting there. It was my special time with him.

I enjoyed Daddy's quiet manner and loved being with him. He brought something of the world into a gray space. He was interested in us, and at dinner always asked about our day. How was school? Who did we play with? What did we do? Even so, it was difficult for me to find a place in the conversation. My brother was forceful and much noisier than I was, and Mom was commanding in her silent withdrawal. Even though feelings were never talked about directly, Mom's and Walt's emotional upsets dominated. It seemed like the one who either had the most trouble or made the most trouble got the most attention.

My brother, Walt, was unmanageable at home, more than my mother could handle. He was also problematic in kindergarten. Recognizing the situation, Dad decided to transfer him to a Yeshiva, even though Judaism was not part of our family life. I think Dad sent him there because it kept him away from home from 7:30 to 4:00. Walt was enraged at being forced to carry an extensive English and Hebrew program. He came home from school angry every day, often throwing temper tantrums. When he calmed down, I would suggest playing a game, never saying a word about his upset. I didn't understand why he had to go that school.

Mom was the only one who cared at all about our Jewish heritage. Daddy wasn't spiritual. In fact, he had no religious beliefs but agreed with Mom that since Walt was attending a Yeshiva, he should have a Bar Mitzvah. I was nine years old, happy for my brother and looking forward to the party. Mom took me to buy a special dress for the occasion, and I was excited to wear it. Still, as the event drew closer and my family's excitement swirled around Walt, I couldn't help but feel overlooked.

The reception took place in a catering hall with live music provided by my Uncle Abe's orchestra. Our whole family, my parents' friends, and all of Walt's friends came to celebrate him. There was a lot of group dancing and musical games, too. I tagged behind the boys, feeling lost and jealous much of the time, wishing some of my friends were with me. My parents were busy with their adult guests, and I don't even remember playing with Aunt Rose. Even Walt didn't care that I was there. I wished the party would end, but it went on and on. Mom must have noticed that I wasn't happy and promised me I would have a big Sweet Sixteen party. She never mentioned it again. Neither did I, and it never happened.

Walt's Bar Mitzvah was the time in my childhood that I felt the most alone and unloved. No one, not even Aunt Rose, ever talked to me about it. My brother always got more attention but it was usually punishments—spankings and yelling. I didn't want that. It was unusual to see him get happy attention. I got little even though I was good.

I think what made me special to Mom and Dad was not my personality or what I accomplished, but how easy I was to raise. I lightened the heavy load that each was carrying. Mom was overwhelmed with Baba and Walt, and Dad was overwhelmed with Mom, Walt, and money concerns. I was neither their focus nor my own; I took my presence and abilities as much for granted as they did. I gave Mom what I thought would relieve her sadness and keep me safe. I felt Dad's heavy burdens and wanted to lighten them, appreciating the little attention he did offer.

The loneliness and invisibility I felt on the day of Walt's Bar Mitzvah became an intense and frequent experience into my adult life as I continued to be an undemanding "good girl."

t w o

AUNT ROSE

ONE POSITIVE ASPECT OF MOM'S DECISION TO MOVE INTO her childhood home was that she could share me with her sister, who more than anything wanted a child. Aunt Rose's love filled me every day. She adopted me as her own and always treated me as her priceless treasure. I never doubted that I was.

Aunt Rose was the angel in my life, providing me with the mothering I didn't have. Unable to have children of her own, she treated me as her daughter. I loved her more than anybody in the world. Every evening when she came home from work, my world brightened. Her hug reassured me that I was loved. Her delight in me made me feel important.

She curled my hair and tied ribbons in it. She taught me how to cook, embroider, and knit. She made pretty sweaters for me, and I always felt beautiful when I wore them, wrapped in her love. When she came home from work I went upstairs to her apartment and we played, cooked, sang, and laughed together. I had my second dinner with her and Uncle Abe, eating off her plate. She loved that I did that while I told her about my day.

There was nothing I said that she didn't want to hear. After my grandmother went to bed, we often crept quietly down the stairs to turn the thermostat higher so that we would be warm. Baba would not allow that. Then I would sit at Aunt Rose's feet while she crocheted, and I knitted or embroidered, asking for help when I needed it. I stayed with her every moment I could until Mom called upstairs to remind me it was bedtime.

Shortly after my tenth birthday, Aunt Rose became ill. I never knew what was wrong with her; she didn't seem sick, just tired. She stayed home from work sometimes, and I was glad she was there when I got home from school. I sat in her room while she slept, reading or doing my homework, waiting for her to wake up. It just felt good to be there.

Her birthday was April 7, and Mom made a special lunch for her. We brought her a tray with a pretty white doily, a red rose in a small vase, a cup of chicken noodle soup, and half of a tuna fish salad sandwich. She was happy and surprised but didn't eat much. Mom took away the tray and asked me to carry in the birthday cake with a big 44 on top. I was proud to do that. Aunt Rose seemed pleased as we sang to her.

Sitting on the bed next to hers, I noticed that her belly was bigger and wondered why. After all, she wasn't eating much and never looked like that before. I got a bad feeling in my stomach.

Six days later, in the middle of the night, I was awakened by a loud tumult. There were strangers in the house, and Mom was screaming hysterically: "Don't treat my sister so rough! Don't take my sister away!" Dad's calming voice was of no comfort. Mom continued to scream. I was very scared and pulled the quilt over my head, frozen in my bed. I knew something very bad had happened. When it was light out I learned that Aunt Rose had died. I don't remember who told me.

My sadness was unbearable, like something inside of me died. In fact it did. The days without her felt empty and long. She was the sweetest part of my life, and she was gone.

At a Long Island cemetery on a cold, damp April afternoon, I stood by myself, far away from where the coffin rested on the cylinders that would lower it. Some chairs had been placed nearby, and several people joined our immediate family to pay their last respects.

My mother was inconsolable, and Dad did his best to comfort her. Nothing helped. I don't remember where Walt was. He was not with me. My Aunt Tillie and Uncle Dave were at the grave, where Baba was making a huge scene, wailing, making loud, scary, guttural sounds. She was pounding her chest and shouting about losing Aunt Rose.

I thought to myself: "You are a fake. You were so mean to her. You killed Aunt Rose. And now you are acting like the saddest of mothers. You are the meanest of mothers."

No one was near me, but I felt my hatred reach all the way across the many gravestones to my grandmother. At least I hoped it did. Feeling so angry with her made it a little easier to be at the cemetery on that miserable day. I wished someone would do something to shut her up. My body hurt all over, and as I looked out at this sham, I felt sick to my stomach.

I stood apart and alone for the entire burial service, wishing my Dad was standing with me, holding me. When it was over, the casket lowered, the few shovels of dirt making a dull thud on the wooden coffin, I silently turned and went to the car to wait for my family to take me home.

Shortly after, Uncle Abe moved away without saying goodbye. No one ever spoke to me about Aunt Rose's death. I couldn't speak about it either, knowing that I wished it were my grandmother, or even my mother, not Aunt Rose who was gone. Life had lost its sparkle for me.

Mom spent more and more time in bed crying. She loved Aunt Rose and missed her dearly. And now she was dealing with her demanding mother on her own. That was more than she could handle. She got so sad that Dad had to take her to the hospital. He told me she was very sick and not to bother her. I heard Dad tell someone that she had electroshock treatments, but I didn't know what that meant. It sounded very scary.

I relived that experience in group therapy twenty-four years later. As we sat in a circle of fifteen, one of the women spoke about her parent's illness. Emotion began to rise in my body; tears filled my eyes and streamed down my cheeks. Feelings surfaced as if they had happened yesterday: "I miss her, I miss her, I miss her. I thought she was going to get better. I miss her, I miss her." My sorrow was profound.

The group supported me as I released some of my long-stored pain that I had buried with her casket on that chilly April day. When my tears eased I felt empty, then calm, and finally peaceful. I felt grateful for the group's love that encouraged me to be open to my grief, again able to feel the invaluable blessing that Aunt Rose was for my first ten years. I was filled with gratitude for the pure joy we had shared. I thank God for her loving presence that lives in my heart every day. I still wear her wedding ring along with my own.

I wish I could have been there with my ten year old, telling her that Aunt Rose would be with her all of her life—that someday she would know that, even though she will always miss her. I wish I could have held her and let her cry as much as she needed to. I would have encouraged her to talk about Aunt Rose, all the things she loved about her, and all the things they did together that made her happy. I wish I could have been there as I am today, or someone else could have been there, to love my ten year old self through her grief.

Thanks to Aunt Rose, I learned early in life that my happiest experience was love. I have spent most of my life desiring to recreate that sustained, sweet feeling within me, to be reciprocated by others.

t h r e e

INTO THE WORLD

SOMETIMES I WONDER HOW DIFFERENT MY LIFE WOULD HAVE been if my mother been able to take my hand and introduce me to the world. Since she was barely able to function, and Dad and Aunt Rose were both working, my brother became my companion and passport when I was eight.

Walt took me out of the grayness of our home and escorted me into playgrounds of fun. But there was a price. I never questioned that accepting his bribes and domination was a better choice than missing out on chances to play in the world. Being away from the darkness and dullness of home was a necessity. Nothing was more stifling than being stuck there. Although I was mad at Walt for his demands, the good times I had made it an easy choice.

Walt would say: "Get me a bowl of fruit or I won't take you to the game." "If you ever tell Mom or Dad, I'll never take you anywhere." "You have to serve me for five days or I won't take you to the movies next week." Sometimes it was three days or seven.

The worst experiences with Walt were the body presses. I

didn't agree to those; in fact, I hated them. He pinned me on the floor and wouldn't let me move. I tried to fight him off but couldn't. Sometimes he sucked on my nose calling it "temptings" while I flailed around helplessly. While not actually sexual, it felt like that. It was scary, violating, and infuriating.

Although I hated Walt's demands, he had another side. He was affectionate, holding my hand in his, taking care that I crossed streets safely. I felt he loved me. He took me with him to his friends' houses and taught me how to play baseball and other games. We played checkers, chess, Chinese Checkers, and card games like Go-Fish, Casino, and Old Maid. He usually won. More than anything, we laughed together. We laughed a lot.

Walt and I did errands to help Mom, and she gave us money for treats. We went to the avenue and had fun shopping together. Sometimes she sent us for delicious thin-sliced Jewish rye bread with tasty black seeds intended for dinner, but we often ate most of it on the way home. Sometimes we bought delectable and beautiful Charlotte Russes, scrumptious round, yellow cakes topped with whipped cream and a cherry. Whipped cream is still one of my favorite foods. Other times we bought chocolate Mello-rolls, ice cream cylinders fitted into waffle cones, creamy and smooth.

We went to the movies many Saturdays, leaving home by noon to see a double feature, newsreel, and cartoon, keeping us away for five or more hours. I saw glamour girls like Lana Turner, beautiful dancing with Ginger Rogers and Fred Astaire, and gorgeous water ballets with Esther Williams. Sometimes the movies were funny with Abbott and Costello, but I was often nervous watching scary mysteries or stories about cops and gangsters. I didn't like those, but it was still better than staying home. Even so, I would ask to leave, but Walt refused, so I closed my eyes and stuck my fingers in my ears. Sometimes I even had nightmares, like after *The Fallen Sparrow* with Peter Lorre, but the cartoons were always great.

The best place my brother ever took me was to Ebbets Field with his friends to see the Brooklyn Dodgers play baseball. We left home in the morning, lunch boxes in hand, and stood on the bleacher line for hours. When the gates opened, Walt's friends, who ran faster than I could, sprinted ahead to get us seats in the front row. They were always nice to me, and we had fun together. I think they found my interest in the game, my enthusiasm and knowledge of the players and their numbers cute—and I could keep score. I always felt that they were happy I was there.

It was such fun to be at Ebbets Field. I was thrilled to be part of a large crowd rooting for the same result. Everyone was on the same team. It felt much bigger than wanting something all by myself.

Those were the years of Jackie Robinson's emergence in Major League Baseball. I was eleven. I will never forget the first time I saw him play. He had quickness and lightning speed. He danced off the bases, teasing the opposing pitcher who never knew when he was going to steal. The best was when he attempted to steal home. The whole stadium stood up screaming with excitement, thrilled when the umpire put his palms down signaling "safe." He was something to see!

Often fans would jeer when Robinson came up to bat, opposing pitchers threw more than usual numbers of balls close to his head, some teammates refused to shower with him, and one even started a petition to ban him from the team. Regardless, he never reacted to provocations and always kept his composure and focus on the game. He shouldered the burden of racial bias with dignity, using his abilities, his will, and his heart to excel in the face of intensely difficult events. I wondered how he was able to do that.

Jackie Robinson inspired me. No one in my life was like him. I had never witnessed such courage, passion, self-control, and excellence. He was a beautiful man—strong and quiet, a man of purpose, determination, and extraordinary talent. He was my hero. I loved him and wanted to be as strong as he was. He knew how to be great even when people dishonored him. It seldom seemed to bother him, and when it did, he used that as fuel to become even greater. Nothing seemed to stop him. I wanted to be like that, and although I didn't know how, he showed me that it was possible. I never forgot that. I still feel blessed to have seen him play. His courage would help me to find my own many years later.

f o u r

ADOLESCENCE

AS A TEENAGER I WANTED TO FEEL BEAUTIFUL AND SEXY MORE than anything. What fun it would be to look like a movie star and be as glamorous as Hedy Lamarr or Rita Hayworth!

I can remember sitting in the vastness and grandeur of Radio City Music Hall when I was ten. The music started playing and lights shined brightly on the stage, as one by one dozens of graceful women came out dancing. They were doing the same step, kicking their legs to exactly the same height at the same time, wearing the same glittery costumes. Then and there I decided that someday I was going to be a Rockette.

Being extremely excited about that idea, I told my Dad the very next morning: "I know what I am going to be when I grow up." He seemed surprised as he looked up from his newspaper and said, "Really? And what would that be?"

"A Rockette!"

He was horrified at my idea and immediately started talking me out of it, giving reason after reason why I couldn't do that. "Smart girls don't do that. Nice girls don't do that. Refined girls don't do that." Clearly he had far different plans for me.

I left the room feeling crushed. Didn't he understand? Dancing is so much fun. Wearing sequined costumes is such a thrill. Being on stage looking gorgeous with so many girls in such a fabulous show was exciting to just think about. I still remember how awesome they looked dancing together, but I never did become a Rockette.

When I was eleven, I went to sleep-away camp. What a joy it was to be with good friends, play all day, dance in shows, and sing in the mess hall. My days were filled with laughter, learning, and happiness. The camp climaxed with Color War when we were divided into two teams and played sports, had songfests, and did "cheeky" cheers after every activity. Bonded as a team, each event seemed so important. I cried the last night of camp, not wanting to leave the fun. I didn't want to go home.

I remember my delight at coming into my grown-up body at age thirteen. I went away to summer camp with the body of a girl and came home with the shape of a woman. I was quite excited about my new body, especially since I had skipped grades twice and was far behind my classmates in my physical development. I enjoyed the rapturous sensations that flowed through me when I lay in bed listening to Martin Bloch's "Make Believe Ballroom." He played a countdown of the top hits each Saturday morning. Nothing matched those feelings, no grades or school honor, no sports triumphs, no community service.

My body and sexuality became my family's focus and battleground. It was a major problem for them. Mom said nothing about my body except that I looked better in sportswear and not as good in "dress-up" clothes. I think she meant sexy clothes. I remember Mom walking naked through our apartment, apparently unselfconscious in front of my seventeen-year-old brother and me. I cringed, wishing that she would cover up and do something about her weight.

Dad was upset that I spent so much time with my friends. He was enraged that I tied up the phone talking with them every evening when he tried to call Mom to say he was on his way home. He often asked, "Don't you ever get enough of them?" He became so frustrated that he finally ordered a second phone line. That was a great victory for me! He was angry about the way I dressed and my interest in my friends and boys. He listened in on my calls and steamed open my letters, which infuriated me. He constantly criticized and accused me of being "unladylike." He seemed to be angry with me all the time.

My weekly Friday night girlfriend movie time sent him into wild outbursts. After the movies my friends and I went to a local diner for hamburgers, fries and cokes. The boys would always show up, being cool, trying to look as if they were meeting us by accident.

Friday nights at the T-Bone Diner were always fun. We played our favorite songs on the jukebox. There was even a little place to dance. I felt beautiful wearing my bobby socks, brown and white saddle shoes, long skirts and "Sloppy Joe" sweaters. I had such a good time dancing and laughing with my friends and these boys who didn't seem like friends but were interesting strangers to explore. We often lingered outside before going home, not wanting to leave. It was usually after 11:00 and time to go home. Although it was past my curfew, it was well worth it.

On my first movie night, I came bounding happily down the hallway to our apartment thirty minutes late. As soon as my father heard my key in the door he greeted me in the foyer shouting, "You floozy, you dirty, no-good whore. I am ashamed of you. You are no damned good. You will never amount to anything. Don't you know that boys are only out for one thing?"

It was as if he threw a boulder at my heart. Too shocked to cry, I stood in the foyer listening to him repeat his tirade, the same words, over and over. Then I shouted back as loud as he did. "You are wrong. You are wrong! I didn't do anything wrong. I didn't do anything wrong! Stop telling me I did something wrong. I didn't do anything wrong!"

Dressed only in his boxer shorts pulled off to the side to prevent exposing himself, he continued berating me. Week after week, he predictably went into the same tirade. Though she was within earshot, Mom remained in their bedroom, silent, while I argued fiercely with him.

Dad became increasingly verbally abusive, constantly berating me. He was totally out of control and completely irrational. Although he never said it, I believe he feared I would become promiscuous, maybe get pregnant and blow my future. He didn't trust me to take care of myself, nor did either of my parents teach me about how to take care of myself. Instead Dad saw my sexuality as bad and dangerous, and he reacted to it with anger.

Surprisingly, Dad never stopped me from going out on Friday night. I continued to go to the movies and to the diner with my girlfriends, had my hamburger and coke, danced, flirted with the boys, and broke curfew. But I always knew what would be waiting for me when I got home. I fought back passionately, holding my ground, but there was no way to win this battle. Eventually I accepted that I must be doing something terribly wrong or my Dad wouldn't have been so outraged. I felt extremely sad that he was so disappointed in me.

Mom acted like nothing was happening. It was impossible for her not to hear my weekly battles with Dad and the abuse he continued to heap on me. Where was she? Why didn't she help me? Why didn't she ever talk to me about those fights? Did she agree with him?

My guess is that Mom thought Dad was wrong, but she felt helpless. Did she ever deal with her own sexuality? Perhaps her sexual shame was so great that she was immobilized. Maybe she was jealous of my body. Whatever the reason, Mom's absence and Dad's aggression wounded me deeply.

Walt had acted as my first boyfriend, taking me out into the world when I was eight. I was thrilled that he did. I was always glad that he was around for Sunday family dinners and TV watching. Big and clumsy as he was, he made me laugh by imitating Ed Sullivan and the little dancing dog acts on that show.

Walt went to NYU, lived at home, and spent lots of his free time there. Little by little, Walt changed. He became overbearing and possessive. I think he felt lonely and hurt that he was no longer the center of my attention and that I was so social, involved with my girlfriends, boys, and parties.

He constantly ridiculed and put down my dates. When Joel took me to the dinner lounge at the Hotel Carlyle, a very chichi nightspot in New York, Walt named him "Joelly Bankrolly." One of my worst memories was when, in a rage, Walt grabbed my arm and pulled me out of the car behind my apartment building while I was kissing my boyfriend goodnight. I was furious and humiliated.

I had the same boyfriend for almost three years of high school. Steve was voted the most popular boy in our class, and I was proud to be his girlfriend. He even gave me his fraternity sweater, maroon and gold with large Greek letters. I was infatuated with him. We went to parties, movies, and occasionally bowling. Sometimes we would kiss goodnight in the stairwell of my apartment building. It wasn't the most romantic spot, with gray, cold concrete surrounding us—but it was private. And every once in a while, when he had the use of his parents' car, we'd find a secluded place to park after a movie. Once, a policeman flashed his bright light inside the car and roughly told us to get moving. I felt startled, scared, cheap, and ashamed. What was I to do with these deep stirrings in my body?

Steve was the first boy that I ever allowed to touch me. We were on the mauve velvet sofa in my apartment as he gently slipped his warm, tender hand inside the keyhole opening in my grey polka-dot blouse. It felt divine. Then I heard footsteps coming down the hall and my heart sank. I jumped up, dashed to one bathroom, Steve to another when my father opened the door. When we returned to the foyer it was obvious that we had been making out. Dad, in a fury, told Steve to leave. He continued to insult and shout at me until I ran to my bed where humiliation and tears overtook me. It later got back to me that Steve told some of his friends what happened that night, greatly adding to my shame and pain.

I often thought, "What happened to my sweet Dad who used to be so happy with me? Why is he so crazy now? I am afraid to say anything to him other than about school. Whatever else I talk about becomes an accusation and argument. There doesn't seem to be anything I do or want to do that is all right with him, except to get good grades. What happened to my sweet Dad? Where is he? And where is my Mom?"

Perhaps not knowing how to handle my budding sexuality, Mom left it to Dad. He didn't know what to do either. How can a man teach a teenage girl about her sexuality? I believe that only a woman can do that. It is a mother's role and Mom was not there.

Mom couldn't deal with my sexuality, and I wish she had sent me to a female therapist, or that the counselor I am today could have been there to help me see that sex was about love, not fear.

f i v e

LEAVING HOME

MOM INSISTED ON GOING BACK TO WORK WHEN I BECAME A high school junior. Dad vehemently disagreed, seeing it as an embarrassment—that Mom's working would be perceived as a sign of his lack of success. Mom stood her ground with surprising strength, and Dad agreed to have her work in his law office rather than take another job. From her first day there she was energized. Her efficiency and ability to connect with and serve clients was a great asset to Dad and a pleasure for her. Her confidence grew quickly. I think she was reliving happy years when she worked as a legal stenographer before she married Dad. I was thrilled to see her functioning so well, becoming more alive. I was also glad for more time alone.

Applying to colleges was a major focus in my senior year. I had very high grades and applied to top ranking Eastern schools, including Cornell where my brother went after transferring from NYU. I had no attachment to the other schools where I applied. Cornell was the only one I had seen. I also had a bigger focus— getting out of the house. Although I was only sixteen, I was ready to leave home. From time to time I thought I would miss my friends, Steve, and our close-knit circle, but the idea of being on my own was exciting.

I will never forget April 15, the day that I received all my college entrance letters. I rushed home from school to find an empty mailbox, but when I went up to my apartment there were four sealed envelopes on my desk. Excited, I ripped open the envelope from Cornell and found I had been rejected!

I put the letter down as tears trickled down my cheeks. That was the only school I had visited and I really wanted to go there. Hurriedly, I opened the letter from the University of Pennsylvania and found another rejection. Even though I wasn't excited about spending four years in Philadelphia, I would rather have been the one to say "no." After these two rejections I was really scared, and I walked away from the desk to look out the window, then quickly circled back to open the letter from Pembroke. Another rejection! By this time I was crying and afraid to open the letter from Tufts, my safety school. When I finally did, I learned that they too had rejected me. How was that possible? I had such high grades. I couldn't believe all four colleges had turned me down! What was I going to do? I had no place to go.

Frantic, I called my Dad's office. Mom answered the phone. Sobbing, I told her, "They all said no." She paused and said: "I know Janie, I am so sorry."

"You know?" I stopped and thought, "How did she know? How could she know? How long had she known?"

As Mom attempted to console me, I looked at the envelopes and saw that they had been resealed carefully. It became clear that my parents had steamed opened and resealed each letter, believing the next one would be an acceptance. I think they held them back so that I wouldn't be disappointed. When the fourth one came, they put them all in a pile and left them for me to open by myself. Why did they do that? I hated that they meddled with my mail, but since they had, why weren't they home when I learned the news? Where were they at a time like this?

At that late date, the best schools to apply to were large mid-western universities with much easier entrance requirements. I chose Ohio State and was accepted within weeks. Even though I didn't know anything about the school, I felt relieved. At least I had someplace to go. Steve was accepted to Lehigh, Lafayette, and Colgate and was pleased with his choices.

By fall I was enthusiastic about going to Ohio State, although a little nervous, not knowing anyone there. I was about to take my first airplane trip, and I left for Columbus by myself. I was so high that I felt I could fly there on my own wings. Looking forward to having space, not dealing with my father's anger, doing what I wanted without fighting for it, all seemed fantastic. Freedom, at last some freedom!

I lived in a house off-campus with fourteen other girls, all from out of state. They came from Wisconsin, Indiana, South Carolina, and New Jersey, each with very different backgrounds. It felt as if they came from foreign countries: what they wore, how they spoke, places they had been. I especially enjoyed the South Carolinians, Rachel and Jeri, whose southern drawls and graciousness warmed my heart. We all liked each other and got along well. Our kind, elderly housemother, Mrs. Neil, cooked our three meals a day and was a sweet and welcoming presence. We spent endless hours in each other's rooms—talking, playing dress-up, borrowing clothes, and listening to music. It was a sisterhood, a happy and lively home in which I felt peaceful and content. It felt like camp. Academics were easy, and there was much time and space to enjoy my newfound freedom.

Shortly after I arrived, I got a call from Steve to tell me that he had enrolled at OSU! He had never even told me that he was applying. I was not overjoyed but rather baffled, unsettled, and upset. I felt ambivalent—cherishing the close, intimate times we had, yet feeling infringed upon since I was looking forward to new adventures. How would I handle my relationship with him? And what would I tell my Dad, knowing he would never trust that this was a surprise to me?

Freshman girls were very sought after by upper classmen. I wanted that experience, wanted to go to parties with them, wanted to be shown the large campus by guys who knew their way around. I wanted to go to football games with them, too. Enormous crowds assembled for these games. People from all over the state came to town; the streets filled with cars, horns blowing; gray and red banners unfurled. And we had a very good team to cheer for—maybe even a Bowl contender! At halftime, a great marching band entertained us, with huge brass and drum sections making complicated formations. It was a grand spectacle as we sang and the band formed an "O" at the ends and "HI" in the middle. O-HI-O!

I dated Steve and many others. A freshman himself, he found that girls preferred to go out with upper classmen. We went out some, but he had a hard time accepting my choice to date others. Through the year it became clear that we would just be good friends, our long history holding us together.

My only contact with home was a compulsory Sunday morning phone call. I brought my parents up to date on my academics, my classes and upcoming exams, while they filled me in on their fairly uneventful lives at home. Rarely was there anything newsworthy about our conversations, and that made it all the more surprising when one morning Dad excitedly said, "Cornell is accepting transfer applications."

Dad was never satisfied with my being at Ohio State, disappointed that I was not at an Ivy League school. He placed a huge amount of pressure on me to re-apply to Cornell, insisting that I take the College Transfer exam. Despite my protests, I took the test, though I hurried through it without care. Months later I was both surprised and disappointed to receive an acceptance from Cornell. I flatly told Dad that I didn't want to go, but he persisted, telling me that I would miss the chance of a lifetime. He said that if I didn't like it after a year, I could return to Ohio State. I was not able to stand my ground in the face of his forcefulness. With no idea how difficult the social adjustment would be to transfer and retransfer, I agreed. Since he was giving me a concession, I thought it was only fair to accept his offer, believing I would return to Ohio State. At the end of spring semester I told Steve that I was transferring to Cornell and, sadly, I never heard from him again.

Even more on my mind was the pain of leaving OSU. I had a wonderful time there: good friends, a happy place to live, interesting classes that were not demanding, some distance from home, and much time to fill with unending opportunities to play. I wanted to stay and was heavyhearted to be leaving. I dreaded saying good-bye to my friends and the life I so enjoyed, and felt burdened with weighty concerns about what lay ahead for me in Ithaca, New York.

s i x

MY FIRST REAL LOVE

THE SUMMER AFTER MY FRESHMAN YEAR IN COLLEGE, WHEN I was seventeen, I worked at summer camp as a counselor and met another boy named Steve. It amazes me how many years later I still think of him and how clearly that summer remains in my memory.

Steve was warm, fun loving, handsome, and smart. He was easygoing, well liked, and had many friends. We were immediately attracted to each other. We had our nights off to play with other counselors, often dancing to the jukebox music in George's, a nearby roadside tavern. I primped before meals every day, feeling beautiful and turned on, anticipating the fun of being together. We had wonderful days off each week, often going to Lake George, walking in the sun, eating ice cream cones, watching the boats, playing and laughing. I cannot remember being as happy with anyone except Aunt Rose—feeling seen, loved, and adored again. Summer romances are notoriously short lived, but I had no doubt that this one was different.

When camp ended I went off to my sophomore year at

Cornell. Steve's life changed dramatically. When his mother died suddenly, his father insisted that he transfer to a New York City college and live at home. Steve did that magnanimously, without complaint. He wrote me beautiful letters daily, and I went home often to be with him.

Those weekend visits were precious to both of us. Despite being good-natured about his situation, Steve was feeling burdened by his father yet obligated to support him emotionally. His grieving father tended to be quite cranky, demanding, and dependent. I could feel the pressure Steve was carrying.

Steve missed being away from his friends and his life at college. Adjusting to a new school was another challenge. Most of his local friends were out of town, but Carol, who lived in his building, was a great support to him. She was a no-frills girl, loyal, and good-natured. It pleased Steve that once in a while we invited her to go to the movies with us.

Our weekend visits were both fun-filled and intense. They allowed us to connect emotionally, to catch up and talk about all that was happening. Being held in his arms and feeling our bodies come alive was delicious.

One warm, sunny spring day we were in his apartment, both thrilled to be alone in a private place. We slowly began to kiss, touch, and gradually take off our clothes one piece at a time. In bed together, I wanted so much to make love for the first time, excited that finally this would happen. The smooth sheets felt so good on my naked body, the warmth of his body so close to mine, his hands and mouth caressing me. Yes, yes, even though it was forbidden, yes. Even though it might be dangerous. Even though... Yes, yes, yes.

The phone rang. Steve got up to answer it.

"Hello, Aunt Nettie, Yes, I am fine. How are you? No, I'm not usually home at this time. (Laughing) You never know what I might be doing."

When the call ended Steve returned to bed. The mood had been broken, the moment was over. He held me gently in his arms and whispered, "I could never do that to you."

I was shattered. Why not? What was wrong with me that I wanted something so wrong?

The daily letters continued, loving, funny, tender, and enthusiastic throughout my sophomore year and into the new camp season. Steve was not there because he had enrolled in summer school to make up for credits lost in transferring. He made plans to visit camp, and we were both eagerly anticipating that time. It would be great fun to go to George's again, play with our friends, and be together where we first met.

Shortly before he was to visit, a letter arrived.

Dear Jane,

I am sorry to tell you that I will not be coming to camp, and will not be seeing you anymore.

I will always remember the good times we shared. I will always remember you as a wonderful part of my life. But it is now time to end our relationship.

I wish you the best always.

With love,
Steve

Stunned, I felt like the blood had drained out of my body. I shed a few tears—very few. It was a grief too large to feel. Frozen, I sat with the letter in my hand. An old feeling came over me, like that day at the cemetery at Aunt Rose's burial. Here was another loss too great to accept. My relationship with Steve was over.

That night I lay alone on the grass, hands clasped behind my head, looking up at the stars, countless stars that now seemed less brilliant, beautiful or magical. How could this be? Why? Why didn't he give me an explanation? How can I accept the extreme change from the letter I received two days ago, filled with excitement and love? What happened?

In my numbed state, I calmly promised myself that I would never love that way again. Never. Never! I kept that promise for a long, long time. Decades.

I buried my sorrow, made it inaccessible. Tearlessly I told our friends that Steve wasn't coming, but I didn't tell them that our relationship was over. Perhaps it wasn't. Perhaps this was just a moment, a moment that would change.

The next day I called my parents. They were both kind and sympathetic. They liked Steve and thought he was good to me and for me. Concerned, they called my brother who was a counselor at another camp quite far away. Walt came to visit me on his first day off. It was unusual, but I felt he really wanted to be there for me. We walked for miles as I told him how shocked and devastated I felt. His presence was comforting, like when I was a little girl and he took me out of the darkness at home. I can't remember another time when he was as caring.

The last weeks of camp were difficult, yet I knew I was better off there than at home. I had many good friends, especially my co-counselor who was always lively and funny. I also enjoyed the campers, sweet kids I had come to love. For eight weeks we were a family, six twelve-year-olds and two counselors. Each night we talked, joked, and laughed as they fell asleep one by one. This family was far more fun than my own.

The last night of camp was bittersweet. The evening activity was held at the waterfront. We sat on blankets on the beach in the moonlight, the dock lined with torches. We sang the same songs that we did in the dining room after meals or on the way to activities or in Color War, skipping across the fields arm in arm. The kids played hard for their teams, yet when they got back to our bunk at the end of the day, we were one team again.

On this last night of camp we each sailed a small paper boat with a candle on it. There were about a hundred candles flickering in the darkness, bobbing up and down as the small waves lapped onto the shore.

Then a trumpet sounded Taps. We all stood up, arms around each other's waists, tears beginning to trickle down our cheeks as we sang:

Day is done, gone the sun

From the lakes, from the hills, from the sky,

All is well, safely rest

God is nigh.

The next night I would be home in my room alone, without these friends, and with no call from Steve.

The camp held reunions every winter in New York City to support the spirit and friendships we all treasured. Afraid that Steve might come and feeling unable to face him, I decided not to go. He did show up, and friends called to report that he asked for me. I wondered what he wanted to say. Did I make a mistake by avoiding him? He could always call me if he chose. He told my friends that his father insisted that our relationship had to end because it was too big a part of his life at that stage and not good for him.

Could that be true? Why would he be so obedient to his Dad? Why didn't he stand for his love? His happiness? It didn't make any sense to me. Yet I sadly realized that perhaps there are things in life that are not meant for me to understand.

I never did hear from Steve. Three years later he married Carol, on my birthday.

CORNELL

DAD AND I DROVE UP TO CORNELL TOGETHER FOR THE START of my sophomore year. As soon as we arrived on campus I could feel his pride in my being a student at this esteemed university. Cornell is a beautiful campus, movie-like with its Gothic architecture covered with ivy, many hills, deep gorges, sprawling lawns, magnificent trees, and neat quadrangles with diagonal pathways. Dad gave me a pep talk about how much I was going to love this place and how fortunate I was to be accepted. I was heavy-hearted and quiet, sorry that I was there, despite Cornell's beauty and prestige.

I was already missing the joy of returning to the school that I had come to love. I had made my way happily at Ohio State, feeling comfortably at home and choosing good friends. Now I was at Cornell and needed to start over again, making new acquaintances with classmates who already enjoyed the bonds from freshman year.

As we sat in the car in front of my massive brick ivy-covered dorm, I felt sad that I hadn't stood up to my father. I had tried but felt worn down by his pressure. Unquestionably he thought he knew what was best for me. I felt weak, angry at myself for submitting and at Dad for never listening.

"Jane," Dad said, as he handed me a beautifully wrapped gift. I pulled apart the decorative paper and lifted the lid of the small box, revealing the watch I had wanted for a long time. It had tiny pearls around a black face with a black suede band. I started to cry, for it felt more like a payoff for my sell-out than a gift. I had fought so hard to state my case, but it always turned out that if I didn't obey my Dad's choices, I wound up feeling wrong or bad.

He had verbally abused me about sex in high school, and now he had pushed me into changing universities because he thought it would be good for my future. Well, what about my present? Didn't that count? It did to me. Feeling powerless, defeated, and angry I quickly said goodbye and went into the dark, intimidating dorm.

My room at Risley Hall was cramped, with a bunk bed, two dressers and two desks. There was one tall, narrow window with small, thick glass panes that allowed little light to enter. Even worse, my roommate was unwelcoming and aloof. Downstairs was a huge cafeteria that served almost inedible institutional meals. Risley Hall was a sad contrast to Mrs. Neil's sunlit house at OSU, where my housemates and I ate dinner together as a happy family every night.

A few days after moving into Risley Hall I got a call from the Cornell chapter of the sorority I had joined at OSU, telling me that there was a space available in the house if I wanted it. My answer, sight unseen, was yes, absolutely yes. What they didn't tell me was that only juniors and seniors lived there. Having gone through two or three years together, these girls had little interest in me and no desire for new friendships. I felt hurt that my housemates didn't seem to care about me, and I blamed them for not telling me the truth when they invited me to live there.

I had little chance to mingle with my classmates, a tight-knit group that lived in a dorm and came to the sorority house only for infrequent meetings. My new roommate was never around since she had a boyfriend with whom she spent all of her free time. It was a lonely time indeed. I felt lost and was not much fun to be around. After living in the house for a while, I decided that sorority economics was the only reason they invited me.

Cornell was cold. In addition to the chill of the sorority house, I braced against howling winds, frigid temperatures, and large snowdrifts. I attended huge lecture classes with little or no contact with my professors, some world-renowned. Although I dated a lot, I still wasn't happy. I didn't embrace Cornell, nor did it embrace me. I felt as invisible and isolated as I did at home after Aunt Rose died. No one seemed to care that I was there. My loneliness at Cornell opened a deep, historic wound. Connection had always mattered most to me and made me happiest. It still does.

I was glad that Walt was in the law school. On Sundays he invited me to his apartment for brunch with his roommates and their girlfriends. We had fun together and talked about dates, parties, campus news, and gossip. When he drove me back to my sorority house he always asked if I had any money. Being treated by my dates most of the time, I usually did, and I gladly gave him my surplus allowance.

Those years at Cornell happened long before I was emotionally aware. I had not yet learned that unresolved pain gets reactivated when circumstances feel similar, adding greatly to present pain. I also didn't realize that I needed to be connected to my feelings and desires before looking to connect with others. It took many years before I understood that I generate and define the quality of my relationships as much as others do.

Still burdened with the pain and anger about Dad's forceful control, I chose child development as my focus. I promised myself that before I had children, I would learn the necessary skills to raise them. Rather than pushing them to do what I believed would be best for them, I would listen, support them, and allow them to lead as much as they were capable.

Dad had no idea what Cornell life was actually like. Jeans were not allowed, curfews were strictly enforced, and housemothers were in charge, but there was a huge amount of drinking. Junior girls were allowed in guys' apartments if there were blue lights on in bedrooms with open doors. On House Party weekends, co-eds were allowed to stay at fraternity houses overnight. I was shocked and humiliated when I innocently turned on the light of the dorm where I was staying and saw most beds occupied by couples. My Dad would have been horrified!

I met Werner, my husband-to-be, in our junior year. He often came to the sorority house to play bridge, an activity that did not interest me. Werner and I often chatted and flirted, and we soon began to date.

I fondly remember springtime of my senior year in Ithaca, when Werner and I went for long rides in the gorgeous countryside. Being a "farm boy" (the most sophisticated farmer you could ever meet), he was aware of country sites and beautiful places far away from campus. We took long drives together, the top down on his convertible, the sun shining and the breeze blowing through my hair. We stopped at lakes and parks, had picnics on blankets in the warm sunshine. I liked being away from campus life, classes, and all the students we were constantly surrounded by—just being alone, exploring, talking about plans, kissing, meandering. Now and then he would stop off at a farm where his family did business, and I would get to see how cows were milked, corn was grown, and hay was baled—all new and memorable times. Werner was attractive, creative, productive, and different from anyone I had ever met.

Our relationship developed happily, going to parties and spending several evenings a week studying together. For the most part we took different courses. I majored in Early Childhood Education; he majored in Business and Philosophy. We had stimulating conversations about psychology and the courses we took in common, literature and government. We took walks, had meals together and made out, but we did not have sex, similar to the limits that many of my sorority sisters talked about setting.

I was very attracted to Werner, but in those years before the pill, pregnancy was my greatest fear, a stigma beyond all. Pregnant girls were sent away from home, hidden by their disgraced families until after they gave birth. They were forced to give babies up for adoption, babies they had felt but were never allowed to see. The shame that pregnancy could create for my family and me was far more than I was willing to risk. Nonetheless, Werner and I had good times and enjoyed being together. Toward the end of senior year we became engaged and planned to be married a year after graduation.

Over time my life at Cornell had improved. In my junior year, many of my classmates moved into the sorority house, and I made friends with some of them. Romance contributed to my growing happiness, yet I still didn't feel that Cornell was my place. People seemed more competitive, grade conscious, and goal directed than I was. Never able to grow roots into that culture, I graduated with a diploma that meant little to me, and I chose never to return to the campus.

Dad's highest value was worldly success. His passionate ambition was intended for my benefit, since he believed that Ivy Leaguers get more respect. Even though that meant far less to me, I followed his script, went to the school of his choice, and would soon marry a classmate capable of becoming highly successful. I was still the consummate good girl.

eight

MARRIAGE, THE PANACEA

WERNER WAS STATIONED IN HARLINGEN, TEXAS, AT AN AIR Force base where he was being trained as a navigator. We were to be married in June, and I would then join him while he completed his three-year Air Force commitment. We spoke on the phone often, wrote letters most days and, while it was frustrating to be apart, we were in close touch.

In the 1950s it was unheard of for a woman to live alone unless she was a spinster or widow. The cultural expectation was that after graduation, I would live with my parents until I married. It never crossed my mind to challenge that. It was not part of my inner conversation nor was it discussed with my friends. To make it even more unthinkable, my older brother lived at home.

There was no compass to navigate through adolescence into adulthood. There was no encouragement for young women to be independent, to explore their desires, abilities, sensuality, and the world on their own terms. There were also few career options. The available choices were teacher, nurse, librarian, secretary, sales clerk or lower management. None of them particularly interested me. In any case I saw career as only a temporary step until I got married.

Marriage was my only solution for three strongly held desires: moving out of my parents' home, guilt-free sexual experience, and security. A man was my answer to acquiring the freedom, pleasure, and safety I wanted.

Having majored in Early Childhood Education, I got a job as a first grade teacher. I had no idea how to begin the school year since the children couldn't read and practical preparation was not part of my college curriculum. Joan, a kind and experienced teacher in the classroom next door, showed me how to put colors, animals, numbers and shapes with corresponding words on the bulletin boards. She was a great help and relief to me. I set out art materials, building toys, and books, all creating an inviting environment. The room looked beautiful on the first day of school—interesting, stimulating, and fun. It was the beginning of a surprisingly satisfying year.

Six-year-old children have astounding curiosity. As the year progressed the growth in their attention span, reading, number recognition, social skills, and group interaction was stunning. It was exhilarating to facilitate their growth. Teaching came very naturally to me and relating to children was also instinctive. I adored my students, and they were happy with me. We enjoyed extraordinary fun and successes together.

Shortly after the school year began, I started to plan my wedding. It was finally my time. When I was nine, I had been promised a sweet sixteen party that never happened. I now made a most uncharacteristic demand: a big bash in celebration of my anticipated liberation.

My wedding took place in June 1957, on a balmy summer

Saturday evening at the gorgeous Park Lane Hotel in New York City. It was an elegant European-style hotel with a gracious lobby, large crystal chandeliers, plush carpets, and doormen and staff suited in brass-buttoned uniforms. A grand and refined place, it was an appropriate venue for my daydream coronation.

At that time, it was customary for brides and grooms to be separated the night before their wedding, but since Werner was flying in from Texas I picked him up at the airport before he went to join his family. I was immediately uneasy when I saw him. He seemed unfamiliar, a person I did not know despite our more than two-year relationship. I thought this was because of our many months of separation. He was unusually lethargic, a vast departure from his typically animated and dynamic self. Exhausted, and without apology, he showed little enthusiasm about our reunion. I was confused and disturbed but excused it, attributing his mood to long hours of travel. Strangely, as I told him about all the exciting wedding plans, he seemed indifferent. I was so absorbed in my dream wedding that I minimized his apathy.

The hotel offered beautiful suites for the bride, groom, and their families in which to dress and relax on the afternoon before the ceremony. Photographers came to take posed and candid pre-wedding photos. When Werner arrived in my suite I was struck by how handsome he looked, eyes sparkling, wearing his white dinner jacket. He was refreshed and revitalized, and his enthusiasm touched, even reassured, me. My big day was here. Months of preparation and concern for detail had come together for this celebration.

Werner's family asked their rabbi to conduct the ceremony since Judaism was important to them. They had fled Germany in 1937 after the Gestapo raided their home, taking all their silver. A few nights later the Gestapo returned and threw a large rock through the front window where Werner normally slept in his bed. Fortunately his mother had moved it after the first intrusion. Although his parents had minimized the danger they had been facing, it was clear that it was time to go. Leaving everything behind and with cash stuffed in his mother's girdle, they left for France in the middle of the night. Fortunately, American relatives had already prepared papers allowing them to come to the United States.

My Uncle Abe's orchestra, the same group that played at Walt's Bar Mitzvah twelve years earlier, performed the music. As they played "Here Comes the Bride," both of my parents slowly escorted me down the long white satin-carpeted aisle. Werner stood waiting for me with the ushers and bridesmaids behind him. I felt beautiful but nervous, comforted to see them all.

Although I was not used to being the center of attention, that night it came easily to me. I danced with Werner, my father, brother and many others, laughing, feeling radiant and playful. My dress, while borrowed, was lovely and low cut with a fitted bodice made of delicate lace. It was a thrill to dance in a long white gown with a billowing skirt. This was indeed my fairytale, a celebration of my freedom.

The flowers were magnificent, mostly white peonies and hydrangeas with freesia. They were everywhere, lining the aisle for the ceremony, covering the altar, and centered on every table. Their sweet scent infused the spacious room, and the music was mellow and pleasant. People danced. Many said the food was wonderful, and it certainly looked delicious, but I was too excited to eat.

I had no sense of time and was so surprised when guests began to say their goodbyes and wish us well. I wanted the party to go on and on. Like Eliza Doolittle in *My Fair Lady*, I could have danced all night! But this was my wedding night, and dancing was just the first part of the celebration.

I wasn't even nervous about making love. We had come so

close many times, and tonight was the night we would finally go "all the way." That phrase echoed in my head. It was such a bad thing to do for so long, that is, until I married. *And now I am married. I have a husband!*

While saying goodbye to some of my friends, Werner approached me and said, "Jane, I just arranged for us to meet my two roommates and their wives at the Half Moon coffee shop a block away."

I thought to myself, "You did what? You didn't even ask me? Both of these guys were ushers and you've been with them all night! How could you want that?" But I said nothing.

He seemed happy with his plan, with no apparent concern for how I might feel about it. My euphoria evaporated instantly. I was shocked and felt as though the blood had drained out of my body. I had no words or energy. Flabbergasted, I thought, "But this is our wedding night. How could you prioritize shooting the breeze with your college buddies rather than be alone with me to celebrate our marriage? Aren't you excited about making love with me, your bride? Did you even consider how I might feel about this?"

I was still in my wedding dress, saying goodbye to friends who were generously expressing their excitement and good wishes, yet inside I was frozen. I acted as though I was happy to receive their kindness while feeling numb and distracted. Internally I had already left the wedding, knowing that my first activity as a newlywed was to go to a local coffee shop. In that nineteen-year marriage, I never again had a moment when I felt extraordinary.

As I sat in the garishly lit coffee shop, my heart ached. Like Cinderella at midnight I came crashing down from the elegance and refinement of Park Avenue to this pedestrian, unromantic setting. I was crushed to be dropped from the spotlight of a joyous gala surrounded by loved ones to being in a place I didn't want to be, with people who meant little to me.

It was very late when we returned to our hotel room. I was heavy hearted, Werner very tired. We went to bed. He quickly fell asleep, while I stayed up much of the night. I thought about the beautiful wedding party in great detail, yet I felt desolate. All the glow and happiness had drained out of me, as if the events of just a few hours ago were in the distant past. I did not shed a tear, unable to grasp what had happened.

We were to return to Werner's Air Force base in Texas early in the morning with no opportunity for a honeymoon. My parents planned to meet us at the hotel and drive us to the airport. I felt uneasy about seeing them, aware of my Dad's discomfort about sexuality. He never would have believed what didn't happen. But then again, neither did I.

EARLY MARRIAGE AND MOTHERHOOD

I WAS FIVE MONTHS PREGNANT WHEN WERNER WAS TRANS-
ferred from Texas and reassigned to Mountain Home Air Force
base in Idaho. We met several couples our age, all college graduates, ROTC officers and their wives, just like us. They were
good company, and many had babies. Life was carefree with no
financial or career advancement concerns, no parents to deal
with and no place to go. The exception was when the siren blew,
signaling either a training mission or an actual conflict situation.
We never knew. Sometimes it would last an hour or two—other
times much longer. Werner would usually come home by the
end of the day, and there never was combat.

Shortly before my due date Werner was injured in a softball
game and required knee surgery. I chose not to give birth at
the Air Force base and we were fortunately able to arrange for
the baby's delivery and Werner's surgery in different New York
City hospitals.

Bill was born a week early. Werner was there for the delivery, but since his surgery was scheduled for the next day, he couldn't visit us in the hospital again. At that time mothers spent a week there after giving birth.

I marveled as soon as I held my baby in my arms, seeing the perfection of his tiny body. As I gazed at my first-born son, the realization that he had lived and grown inside of me was miraculous! I had felt his first flutter of movement and now I would tend to him every moment of every day.

On my first day home I was excited to be able to visit Werner, surprised and thrilled that my body was almost back to its normal appealing size and shape so quickly. I felt beautiful, wearing a lovely fitted white eyelet, off-the-shoulder dress and high heels. I was happy to be seeing my guy and couldn't wait to show up looking trim, like myself again.

I was eager to show Werner pictures of our beautiful son, but he showed little interest. I backed off to gather myself, trying to handle my disappointment. This was our first baby. After being apart for over a week, why was he so distant? A few minutes later he said, "Maybe you shouldn't come here too often. My roommate doesn't have a wife nearby, and I don't want him to feel lonely." Devastated, I left his hospital room soon after. Why was he being so cold to me, and why was he not interested in hearing about our baby? When I got into my car and was alone, I allowed my tears to flow.

Soon after, we returned to Idaho. Werner often came home at odd hours after flights and woke Bill up to play, interrupting his sleep schedule. He also became demanding of my attention. Inconceivable as it was, I began to think he was jealous of my involvement with our baby. It almost felt like I had two children vying for my attention.

Motherhood came naturally and easily to me after the initial months of sleeplessness, being on call around the clock. My time with Bill was a joy. Holding him, feeding him, singing to him, just looking at him and making scrapbooks of captioned photos made me happy. I was surprised when I went in to check on him and saw he had turned over for the first time, and later when I heard him calling and found him standing, proudly holding onto the crib bars. We had sweet and playful times together.

After several months of daily baby care, I asked Werner to take charge for a day so I could have a break. Boise was about an hour away, and it would be a welcome change for me to be in a city on my own, to roam the shops and relax. He agreed.

It was exhilarating to drive out on the open road and take a deep breath. An immediate sense of freedom washed over me, with no one else to tend to or prioritize. Going at my own pace and listening to my own rhythms felt both strange and delicious. Wandering through the shops was a treat, and eating lunch uninterrupted felt like an extravagance. I longed to have a close girlfriend to play with, but reminded myself that this day was a gift in itself.

The return trip seemed longer. I was tired, and could feel a growing tension, concern about how Werner was doing. Was he being attentive and watchful? When I arrived home and opened the door, a strong stench greeted me. I found a chain of dirty diapers snaking around the floor. I was so let down that I never asked for a day off again.

Just after Bill's first birthday, Werner was discharged from the Air Force and we moved back East, where life changed dramatically. We decided to live in White Plains, a suburb of New York City. I didn't know anyone there but chose this city as a convenient and pleasant place to live, midway between our parents. I was happy with our apartment and excited to create our first permanent home.

Werner got a job on Wall Street, training to be a stockbroker. He was very enthusiastic about it and once licensed, spent four nights a week calling prospective clients in California after his workday. He was an excellent salesman and quickly built a sizable clientele. Bill and I were together day and night, and I often felt lonely after he went to sleep. When Werner came home he was exhausted, needing to unwind and sleep, too.

A few weeks after settling into our apartment, I introduced Bill and myself to Elin, a woman sitting in the neighborhood park tending her ten-month-old daughter Shelley. We became good friends, moms together. We walked, talked, had lunch, window-shopped, went to the park, and had indoor play dates with our children. Eventually we included our husbands, and the four of us got together on many weekends. Years later, with our growing friendship and their respect for my mothering, Elin and Bob asked if I would be guardian of their children in the event of a common death. With Werner's agreement, I accepted.

Bill was three when Dick was born. Dick was an adorable baby, easy-going, calm, and happy. He was quite large and chubby, with fair skin, a big dimple, and sparkling blue eyes. The apartment was small for the four of us so I began house hunting and found my dream house. Within six months we moved into a beautiful Dutch Colonial home in Rye, New York. The neighborhood, called Greenhaven, was so exquisite that I naively believed everyone who lived there must be happy.

Actually my first winter there was abysmal—lonely, cold, and dark. No people were visible except as they passed by in their cars. I was extremely isolated, at home with a three-year-old and an infant requiring constant care, and a husband working late four nights a week. I could see that Bill was finding it difficult to accept the time I gave to his brother. He was used to my undivided attention. Fortunately, Werner's growing income allowed us to hire a mother's helper, affording me more time for Bill and some personal space in my days. I was so grateful. In the spring I became active in the community and spent many enjoyable years building strong bonds with other young mothers and their families.

Bill's capacity to focus amazed me as he independently spent hours building garages and playing with his collection of cars and trucks. Dick grew into a sunny, fun-loving, lively toddler. Often exuberantly joyful, he ran into the kitchen grinning from ear to ear, announcing himself: "Here comes Gickie!" I was touched by his sweetness and playfulness. I had fun with both of them, loved them and felt loved by them.

I still longed for the experience of raising a daughter. Werner wanted a large family, so we decided to have another child. Two years later my third son, Barry, was born, which took some accepting. Yet when I saw him I softened, happy and grateful for my beautiful boy. He was born two weeks early while Werner was away on a business trip. Elin and Bob took me to the hospital.

Barry showed his mischievous and curious nature early. He experienced things fully, becoming a Native American dressed in costume or a baseball player in his uniform for weeks, sometimes months on end. When in kindergarten he walked around the house blindfolded to know what life was like for his blind classmate, Nicky. His experimentation always fascinated me yet sometimes was a great challenge.

I loved being their Mom. I wanted each of them to know how important they were to me and that I was there to listen to them. I wanted to know what they were interested in and was fascinated watching their unique personalities develop. I was delighted to give them the love Aunt Rose gave me daily for the first ten years of my life.

Still wanting a daughter, I decided to try one more time. Two and a half years later Susan was born. The doctor woke me in the recovery room to tell me I had a girl. I didn't absorb that until I got to my room where I was overjoyed to finally see a pink telephone. Pink buntings, gold diaper pins, and ruffled outfits poured into our home. Friends and family generously rejoiced with us.

Life for Susan was difficult in our male-dominated household, with three older brothers who excluded her from their play and a Dad who didn't know how to relate to a girl. I suggested enrolling her in dance and gymnastics but she wanted to do what her brothers were doing, primarily play sports. She clung to me for connection and protection while trying as hard as she could to be included by them

When Susan was eight I took her to a gentle and attentive male therapist. I wanted her to have loving adult male attention, while denying that I was longing for that myself. Happily she thrived in his company and through time found strength in her feminine self, in school and sports with her friends.

I learned that the greatest reward of raising children is seeing them thrive. Motherhood is a selfless role that draws deeply from a woman's nurturing capacities. It requires giving, guiding, and supporting, qualities that are undervalued and that receive too little recognition in our culture. Learning to give loving energy on call all day, every day—week after week, month after month and year after year with little respect—challenged me to give that honor to myself. For me, motherhood is a deeply spiritual path.

t e n

WERNER'S EARLY
WORK LIFE

WERNER'S SUCCESS IN GOING FROM TRAINEE TO ACCOUNT
executive in his Wall Street firm was impressive, but the level
of responsibility he carried felt heavy to him. He was more confident in his sales ability than the financial information from
which he was making recommendations. He struggled with that
dilemma for two years and thought about changing his career.
He spoke to his college roommate, who had started his own
investment firm with two other men, and offered to recommend
that his clients transfer their funds to that firm for management.
His roommate urged him to come to work for them, assuring
him that he would then feel confident in the investment research
he would have available. Werner decided to give it a try.

Early on he and a workmate realized that investor interest in mutual funds was growing rapidly and that they could
significantly increase their income by building relationships
with institutional fund managers. At that time the commission

percentage on transactions for a 100,000-share order was exactly the same as for a 100-share order.

I have a vivid recollection of the two men, excited as children, sprawled on our living room floor with a large map of the United States. They were divvying up territories where large mutual fund headquarters were located, anticipating the value they could add and the gigantic commissions they would earn from serving these institutions. Werner chose to start with Minneapolis and Kansas City; his workmate took Boston. They methodically met with fund managers, building relationships and trust, and in a short time their production skyrocketed. Both became partners in their fast-growing Wall Street firm.

Werner was excited about his new work and traveled most weeks. He encouraged me to be present in his work life, seeing me as a social asset, easily and naturally forming relationships to support his professional connections. His work included entertaining clients and afforded us occasional weekend trips to luxury hotels in beautiful places. We both enjoyed these business events. It was a wonderful balance to my daily life with our children. I was so grateful for our extraordinary live-in mother's helper who made my involvement possible.

After a while we invited some of Werner's clients to our home when they came to New York. Jimmy and Frank were frequent visitors and became good friends of mine. I appreciated that Werner brought this richness to our home.

One of my highlights of his career was a trip to the General Motors Building while it was under construction. Werner's firm had rented space high up in the fifty-story skyscraper, overlooking Fifth Avenue and Central Park in Manhattan. It was breathtaking to enter the skeleton at night and ride a crude elevator up to its heights before any interior walls were constructed. I was filled with awe as I took in the beauty of the magnificent buildings bordering Central Park, a stark contrast to the rawness of this immense structure. Standing high above Manhattan on wood planks over concrete floors with bare light bulbs dangling from exposed wires was an unforgettable experience. The memory still brings a smile to my face every time I pass the building.

My hope was that, as the children grew more independent and Werner's business required less energy, we would become closer. During these years, in addition to caring for our children, I created and maintained many lasting friendships, participated in community service, supported Werner's career, and created a satisfying social life for us. Yet as time went by I became more and more lonely. My life was rich in many ways, but I didn't have a devoted marriage partner or an involved co-parent.

Werner spent most of his time working or watching sporting events with the kids. He saw his responsibility as earning money. Home was his place to rest and recharge. He did his "R & R" and slept much of the weekend. I felt angry. He traveled a lot. I felt lonely. He spent Sundays watching double-header football games. I felt left out. He didn't help out at home. I felt put-upon. Yet I minimized those feelings to myself and rarely expressed them directly to him.

The last time I remembered crying was when I was at LaGuardia Airport to meet Werner returning from a business trip. I saw a sailor and his girlfriend running toward each other from about thirty yards apart. They ran as fast as they could, arms outstretched as they approached each other, and stood in a long, loving embrace. I didn't question why I was crying, but there was never such a greeting when my husband came home.

I couldn't understand why our marriage had become so humdrum. It was either this to-do list or that, this arrangement or that obligation. What happened to the romance, the playfulness and adventure that we had at Cornell? Where was the sexual connection that was so palpable yet forbidden then? Was it the challenge of prohibition that turned him on? It certainly didn't seem to be me.

After ten years, Werner became disenchanted with his Wall Street life. After a decade of intense travel and work, he lost his passion for it. The SEC drastically cut commission percentages on institutional orders. Top management of his firm was close to acquiring a well-known, established brokerage house that was in financial trouble. Werner was opposed to that decision, believing that the effectiveness and efficiency of their small firm would be compromised. His meteoric success from trainee to partner had earned him enough to consider retiring at age thirty-five.

The same partner who helped map out the mutual fund sales effort all those years ago invited me to lunch. He begged me to use whatever influence I had to convince Werner to take a leave of absence rather than bail out. He explained that the upcoming expansion would be worth huge amounts of money, and that the firm would no doubt accept his temporary leave. He said that if Werner resigned he would lose that life-changing opportunity.

I appealed to Werner to remain affiliated and take some time off to see what he wanted to do next. Although his partner had convinced me that he had nothing to lose by taking a temporary leave of absence, Werner disagreed, convinced that they were making a colossal error in expanding the firm. I wondered whether his decision to leave wasn't at least partially based on feeling slighted when his partners didn't listen to him. He decided to resign from the firm, sold his shares and retired. As it later turned out, he left millions of dollars behind.

eleven

ITALIAN SUMMER

IN 1970, RETIRED, LOST AND DEPRESSED, WERNER DECIDED that it would be a great idea to take the family to Italy for the summer. I was thrilled with the prospect, never having been to Europe. Months in advance, he went off to scout out a summer home for us and found a beautiful villa in Ansedonia, a small town 130 kilometers north of Rome. It was on the west coast, situated at the top of a hill overlooking the Mediterranean. Built of stone with a large terrace, it had a lovely garden filled with fruit trees and flowers that lined pathways to the sea. The photos he brought home were gorgeous.

In June he went to Germany to pick up our new Mercedes and drove to Milan to welcome our four children, our mother's helper Rachel, and me. The five-passenger car was crowded with seven of us, and the drive to our villa was long. Susan, who tended to get carsick, slept on the back ledge. Rachel sat in the rear with three children. After a while Bill moved up front, and I was so exhausted that I sat curled up on the floor and fell asleep resting my head on his leg.

When I awoke, the views were breathtaking! The beautiful colors of Italy, ochre, green and sienna, the sand and the rocks, the peace, and the sun all immediately touched me. We passed long stretches of gorgeous yellow sunflower fields, their faces looking up to the heavens in unison. During our several rest stops I enjoyed the language, the music, the food and wine, the laughter and the obvious love of children. I felt as if I had landed in paradise, and when I saw the home we were to live in, I was convinced I had.

Life was very different in Italy, leisurely and pleasure-filled. There were no supermarkets; simple little shops opened in the morning, closed for siesta, and reopened late into the evening. I went to town daily to buy fresh bread, fruit, cheese, fish, and vegetables. I became friendly with shopkeepers and restaurant owners who were delighted by our four children. The townspeople were excited to know Americans. They happily and gently expanded our vocabulary, encouraging us to speak their language.

We hired a high school girl to teach the children Italian. She conversed with them in English and Italian and brought them first grade primers to study. An elderly woman came weekly to make us fresh pasta: fettuccini, spaghetti, ziti, and wonderful fresh tomato sauces. Italian tomatoes are simply divine!

Werner spent much of his time alone, reading and doing crossword puzzles, and also playing board games or cards with the kids. I explored the town and the language, spending most of my time with the children and Rachel. She was a beautiful and kind young woman who felt like the little sister I wished I had. She lived with us for several years, was a part of our family, and loved the children and me. She also added some humor to our Italian trip since a young man down the road, whom we nicknamed "Franco Spaghetti," was quite interested in her.

Dick, who was nine at that time, became our Michelangelo expert and guided us to see not only the famous Pieta in the

Vatican but less visited sculptures like Moses, housed in a remote church in Rome. We took day trips to Florence and saw the great David and the Duomo. We walked along the Ponte Vecchio over the muddy Arno River. I was thrilled with magnificent art museums and shops selling fine papers and leather goods. We went to Pisa to see the Leaning Tower. Our twelve-year-old son Bill took an amusing photo of the tower standing vertical with the people leaning. Adorable! We went to Naples and Orvieto, and we took an unforgettable trip to Venice. We fed the pigeons in Piazza San Marco, heard music everywhere, watched adept gondoliers maneuver through crowded canals, smelled delicious food aromas wafting into the alleyways, and walked narrow streets lined with beautiful shops. I was enthralled with Italy and its culture: warm, friendly, musical, and alive. To this day it is still my favorite destination.

My rich outer life in Italy made me even more conscious of the emptiness in my marriage. It felt lifeless except when we were sightseeing or out to dinner as a family. My hope of becoming closer to Werner when the pressure of his work life lessened was shattered. There was no friction between us, but there was no sparkle either; no satisfying emotional connection or sexual intimacy, no conversation about what either of us was feeling or desiring. I felt his restlessness and was relieved when he decided to take an unneeded weeklong trip to New York in July.

It was a defining time for me. My ideal Italian lifestyle was far beyond anything I ever imagined, yet I felt disconnected from my husband. The disparity was obvious. Although it was too scary to embrace, it was far too great to deny.

t w e l v e

GOING INWARD

WHEN WE RETURNED HOME, MY MARRIAGE FELT AS LONELY in Greenhaven as it did in Italy. Times with my children, friends, and community were satisfying, but time with Werner was most often emotionally depleting, disappointing, and unromantic.

I began to question why that was true. Werner was more comfortable in the business world where he primarily used his intellect. He felt in control in his work life and was safe and secure in his superior position. His peers, clients, and workmates were all men except for a few women in support roles. As in his childhood family and in our marriage, women were needed yet seen as less important than men. I observed that once Werner won the prize he was pursuing, he immediately began his quest for the next one. His work life had satisfied that drive; committed relationship did not.

Feeling lost and restless since his retirement, Werner had traveled from Italy to Australia for a month to see what life there was like. Clearly he was searching for something. When he returned he started attending encounter groups at the Casriel

Institute. Although we had many conversations about psychology when at Cornell, they were academic. Neither of us had ever been in therapy. I never thought about it and was surprised yet pleased when he began attending group sessions, hoping he would return to his former energetic self.

The Institute encouraged expression of deep emotion, yet as he continued his group sessions, he became increasingly depressed. He stayed in bed and read psychology books most days. He didn't shave or want to go out, and he didn't participate in any family activities. I became increasingly concerned and, as time went on, quite frightened about his condition. I wanted to understand what he was doing and asked to go to a group. He was pleased with my interest and agreed to take me to my first inner journey experience in December 1970.

I was surprised at how scared I was. We stopped for dinner at a local hamburger place. I was unable to eat, my stomach churning, mouth dry and hands sweating. He was excited.

We were assigned to separate groups. I was led to a small nondescript windowless room with bare beige walls and a dark grey carpet. The group leader was already sitting in the circle on one of the seven padded metal chairs. While I don't remember her name or what she looked like, she seemed soft and gentle, and she welcomed me warmly. Soon after, five other women joined the circle and the session began.

A woman sitting diagonally opposite from me asked to share about an incident that happened with her father. All of us listened in rapt attention as, in tears, she went into detail about his cruelty and insensitivity. The leader asked her some probing questions that she answered, expressing even more intense pain. Before long, she was sobbing. I found myself crying too, thinking that my tears were about her and her story. Gradually her tears ebbed and when she finished I sensed a deep peace in her and quiet in the room. I didn't understand why she felt better or why the energy in the room felt lighter.

The group leader then approached me and asked why I had been crying. I told her that I was upset, feeling sad for what I just witnessed. She said she understood and asked me to tell the group about my father. Before I knew it, I was revealing my father's vicious, repetitive verbal abuse about my sexuality during my early adolescence.

I was surprised at how easily and naturally I spoke, telling these strangers my darkest secrets. I hadn't cried for many years and was astonished by the depth and intensity of my emotions.

Dad was my primary parent because of my mother's ongoing depression. He was usually a loving and supportive father to me until my body changed at age thirteen. After that, my sheer presence seemed to throw him into a state of disapproval and fury.

The more I talked, the more I understood. His damning words were so different from the kind and attentive man whose face lit up years ago when he saw me. His huge turnaround tore me apart. I felt like I had no parents. One had become abusive and disapproving, and the other was absent.

There was a silence in the room when I finished telling my story. I remember the group leader's eyes, kind and clear looking into mine, silently encouraging me to continue letting out my pain. Kneeling on the floor in front of me holding my hands in hers, she reassured me: "This is good Jane, this is good." The five other women surrounded me, also urging me to let go and go deep into myself to purge those condemning words and the hurt they caused. As I spoke of those devastating events, I felt better and lighter, just as the woman before me had, like a weight was being taken off my heart.

Those moments in that room changed my life forever. Nothing seemed as compelling as reopening those painful memories that I believed I could never endure. I now understood the enormous impact of carrying my Dad's beliefs inside me since adolescence, that my sexuality was bad and that I would never amount to anything in the world. My need to be loved as the "good girl" he wanted me to be was a tragedy at my own expense, leaving me with sexual guilt and doubts about my worthiness. I had never before been that honest with myself.

I learned that day how accepting my Dad's beliefs had blocked me from my genuine self, and that my truth lay dormant within me. By releasing those memories I took a giant step toward my freedom. Now I was asking the questions that had never occurred to me before, questions my "good girl" self would never deign to ask. I couldn't wait to find out what else was blinding me.

One evening, three months after I started group therapy, Werner came into our family room where I was watching TV and said that he wanted to talk to me. Seeming unusually quiet, maybe even nervous, he sat down and said, "Jane, my group leader told me I need to tell you something that I have been hiding for years. During our engagement, while I was in Texas and you were in New York, I was having sex with other women." Before I could ask him anything about that, he went on, determined to tell the whole story. "I have continued to be with other women throughout our marriage. I want you to know that none of them ever meant anything to me."

I felt a surge of pain through my body and then it went numb. My mind traveled back to our wedding night, when Werner chose to be with his friends in a coffee shop rather than crowning our beautiful wedding by making love. He had been directing his sexual energy and attention to other women all these years. Why?

Although he seemed relieved to have emptied his guilt I was devastated, feeling both betrayed and rejected. All the emotions that surfaced in the face of such deception overwhelmed me: pain, rage, fear, and great insecurity. Questions flooded my mind. What does that say about him? What did that say about my sexuality? What does that say about his? How can I ever trust him? Who were these women? Did I know any of them? Was he emotionally involved with any? After all, he had kept his infidelity from me for the entirety of our marriage. Was he capable of lying about emotional involvement too? I was not convinced by his attempt to reassure me that he was not.

I didn't want him to touch me, couldn't meet him eye to eye, and grieved about it for months. Focusing on mothering was grounding, friendship was soothing, and community, stabilizing, but carrying on what appeared like a normal life was agony.

Sexuality became my focus in group therapy. I had interpreted his choices as meaning that I wasn't enough, that I was inadequate. But even if I was, why didn't he suggest working it out together rather than splitting off? My group leader assured me that the issues were his, both sexual and emotional. I didn't fully accept that, nor did I know how to sort it out. Not having had experience with other men, I didn't know much about my own sexuality. I did know that I hadn't found our sex life satisfying, but I had never expressed that. Now in addition to sexuality, my most pressing issue was trust.

I attended these groups for about a year and a half. It was such a relief to be emptying the huge pockets of grief I had held inside. For weeks members encouraged me to express my anger in the safety of the group. Finally, I unloaded frustration and outrage that I didn't even know existed. After each release I felt lighter and stronger, less powerless and less victimized.

Tension ran high in our household as we started group couple therapy. I was encouraged to express my anger directly to Werner who, to his credit, received it openly. It was a temporary relief but it didn't change the core issues of our relationship: trust, sexuality, control, and dependence. I was grateful for group therapy that offered me the safety to let go and feel deeply, but I decided that I needed a one-on-one process to focus on my individuality and work toward some resolution in my marriage.

When I shared this idea with Werner he agreed that it would be a good idea for each of us and began to research varying therapy modalities. He recommended bio-energetics, a mind-body-emotion process. I read about it and decided that even though this was an innovative idea that would definitely be a stretch for me, it might be a more direct route than traditional talk therapy.

I began working with John, a bio-energetic psychiatrist. In my first session he asked me to stand barefoot in my lingerie with my arms outstretched and hands pointed upward in front of me. Even though I was uneasy, I went with it. He approached me, fully dressed in shirt, tie and slacks, pushing against my palms. I fell back. He did it again and I fell back. Repeated again and again with the same result, he said, "Pushover, eh. Pushover." The therapy had begun. It was excruciating.

It surprised me how much I was focusing on myself—and how glad I was about that. A new me! From my first group session on, I received profound loving support, and I was gaining strength and meaningful awareness. I leaned on my mother's helper to offer some of the attention that I had been giving to my children, accepting that it was healthy to now give some of that energy to myself. I believed that, in the end, it would be good for them, too.

I even became grateful to feel my pain, for once it was expressed I felt so much better. With each release of emotion and each insight gained I felt stronger. Even with the serious issues around Werner surfacing—his infidelity, my anger at him, and my sexual insecurity—I felt happy that I was giving myself the attention I needed. These were my first steps toward looking inside and learning to be what I would come to call soul selfish.

In several subsequent sessions John continued to prod me to contact my assertion. Again, with me dressed in my lingerie, he jabbed and poked at me. He nudged and bumped me, urging me to stand for myself. I was paralyzed. Time and again I burst into tears, feeling helpless. After many similar sessions, he finally provoked me enough to engage.

Tauntingly he said, "Good girl. Good girl. Oh, you are such a good girl." In a flash I could hear my mother's voice: "You are such a good girl." That was the biggest compliment she ever gave me. "You are a good girl and not demanding."

Familiar "good girl" childhood thoughts and images flooded my mind:

I peek into Mom's darkened room. She is in bed again, sad and tired.

I will be good and quiet and not bother her. I won't ask for anything.

I'll make sure I don't cause any trouble.

Maybe she is sick. I don't want to make her even sicker.

What would happen to me if she got worse because of me? Maybe Walt's bad behavior will do that. What would happen to us if it does?

I don't know what to do. I just want my Mom to get better.

An unbearable sadness overcame me and John moved forward. I collapsed onto the floor weeping. He tenderly cradled me as the child I was in that moment, crying from my core. We silently sat that way for several minutes, after which I knew I was different, exhausted but different. I had passed through three decades in that session.

In my next weekly session John's prodding began as usual, but

I was able to meet him. I was alive and in the present—energized, laughing, jabbing back, spirited and strong. It was now a game, and I was free to play!

I quickly learned the ways that I submitted to others: their needs, preferences, and desires. I also saw how difficult it was for me to know what I wanted, to express my wishes or stand up for them in the face of disagreement.

John began to focus attention on my anger. I could accept my sadness but often collapsed into it rather than expressing my rage. Assertion was not available to me even in circumstances that would ordinarily be considered provocative: unfair sharing of responsibilities, broken promises, and neglect.

In another session, John asked me to lie down on a bed and start kicking my legs. He asked me to tell him about my Mom. As I was kicking I told him that I was mad about dancing around Mom's constant tears and the heaviness she brought to our family. Mad at how little she did. Mad that she needed so much. Mad that she paid so little attention to anything about me other than that I didn't make trouble. Mad that she didn't compliment me on my excellent report cards and skipping two grades. Mad that she wasn't ever there to play with me.

I kicked and kicked. I flailed my arms. By this time I was shouting, "I am angry, I am angry." He kept urging me on: "More, more, there's more in you. Keep telling me how angry you are at your Mom, keep showing me how angry you are." I am mad that she didn't ask what I wanted and liked. Mad that she didn't stand up for me as a teenager when my Dad shouted and called me a whore who would never amount to anything. Mad that she never told me how beautiful my body was. Mad that she was so fat. Mad! Mad! Mad!

John was correct. There was far more anger in me. I kicked and shouted for a long time. It seemed endless but slowly my fury began to subside. As it ebbed it felt like I was floating on a magic carpet with small comforting undulations: easy, soft, swells moving up and down. With my eyes closed, my body relaxed and open and my senses aware, it felt like I was gliding through space, deliciously light and empty.

After about a year of these sessions I wondered if there was anything more to me than the results of a heartbreaking marriage and childhood experiences and beliefs that caused me pain. Was I simply the sum total of my past, a product of my well-meaning but unaware parents? If not, who am I? Is there an end to this processing? Will I ever find my real self?

While still stuck in darkness and scared of where all this was leading, there were moments of hope. I was happier being an adventurer and putting myself on the line. Inner blocks were beginning to melt as I expressed my feelings and connected with my body. Release felt better than fear, and risk was better than paralysis. I could see glimmers of light, the beginnings of a new version of myself. Even though I wavered between fear and optimism, I knew there was no turning back.

t h i r t e e n

DAD'S LAST DAYS

DAD LOVED HIS WEEKLY VISITS TO MY FAMILY HOME. IT FUL-
filled his every picture of what I should be, do, and have. He was
delighted with the "American Dream" that I was living. I had
a beautiful Dutch Colonial house with double doors, latched
hardware, and wide planked pegged floors. It was sturdy and
authentic, located in a gorgeous neighborhood bordering Long
Island Sound. I had a handsome and prosperous husband and
four healthy, bright, beautiful children. I could feel his pride in
me. It was as though my life made him feel successful.

My parents came to visit almost every Sunday, laden with
goodies from New York City. We had a ritual of afternoon dessert,
and they stayed until the children's bedtime. Dad played ball with
the kids in the yard or games in the family room. He always went
for take-out dinner, wanting to make it easier for me.

Eight years after we moved to Rye, Dad became ill. He noticed
blood in his urine and within days was taken to the hospital for
testing. He was diagnosed with prostate cancer that had spread
to his bones.

The morning after the diagnosis I put on a bright colored dress to visit him, wanting to look and feel as cheerful as I could. When I got there I was relieved to see that he was alone in his room, sitting in a chair reading the newspaper. He did not look up as I greeted him and sat directly across from him. I waited quietly for him to speak, but he didn't. He sat there, his face hidden by his open newspaper. After a few minutes, I finally said, "Dad, I know."

He slowly lowered the paper and, tears streaming down his cheeks, apologized for crying. I was crying, too; I reached out to hold his hands, telling him that I was so sorry.

It was excruciating to watch him shrink to a shadow of himself, visibly dropping weight week by week. Dad was like a different man, his voice weak and his presence frail. He was in and out of the hospital several times.

My mother was not able to nourish him either physically or emotionally. Visiting them at home one day at lunchtime, I was infuriated to see her serve him SpaghettiOs from a can—for a man who needed all the nutritional support possible.

The next time Dad was taken to the hospital he was delirious, making wordless sounds, extremely restless, flailing around in his bed, kicking off the covers and exposing himself. Alarmed, I stood in the corner far away from him while he repeatedly screamed, "Janie, get away from me." The nurse came in and gave him a sedative to calm him. I went to his bedside and stroked his hand until he fell asleep.

Until his last days, Dad wanted to come to our home on Sundays. Since he could no longer drive and Mom was too upset, they took the train. During one of his last visits he sat quietly at my kitchen table while I prepared dinner. He apologized that he couldn't bring dinner in. I was standing at the stove cooking, and we were chitchatting about how the kids were doing in school. Then he changed the subject and whispered, "I'm sorry, Janie.

Sorry for the way I treated you growing up."

I continued to cook with my back to him, frozen, unable to face him. My heart was racing, and in panic and emotional flight, I made light of his apology. I quickly said, "It's OK, Dad. You can see it's all OK now."

The conversation was over, but I had lied. Despite that life-changing day at the Casriel Institute, I was not able to reveal my pain or the impact of his attacks directly to him. I was too frightened to go back into that time. I prevented myself from touching that pain again, not knowing what would come out if I did. I told myself that he was too frail, too sick, and too old to deal with the truth.

His verbal abuse still lived in my memory, and I couldn't be honest with him. I didn't want to hurt him. Later that evening I realized I was unable to give him the space to ease his guilt and pain, something I think he wanted to do before he passed.

Dad was gravely ill. Mom was at his side day and night. The last time he was in the hospital he fell into a coma. He was totally quiet. I held his hand and asked him if he knew that I was there. He blinked his eyes, and I decided that was his yes. He remained in the coma for several days then peacefully passed. I was relieved that he was out of his pain and misery. He hadn't been the man I had known for a long time. It had been a very difficult road for more than two years.

Several years later I relived my kitchen conversation with Dad in a role play with a therapist. This time I told my truth. From the beginning, my father could not handle my vibrant sexuality. It created huge anxiety in him. His continual verbal abuse caused me so much stress that after a while I thought of my sexuality with more pain than pleasure. I decided it was safer to put a lid on those feelings. That decision greatly diminished my sense of beauty and power as a woman. Sadly, not honoring my own femininity shaped my choice to marry a man who did not honor it either.

I don't know if, on that day in my kitchen, Dad knew that I was lying. I am hopeful that my authentic forgiveness, even though given years later, freed him wherever his soul was resting in the Great Beyond. I will always love him.

fourteen

SPAIN: THE BEGINNING OF THE END

THE BREACH OF TRUST CAUSED BY WERNER'S INFIDELITIES never completely healed, but I continued to work on myself to let go of it. I was hopeful that my pain would ebb, and that we could resurrect our marriage. With that desire in mind, I agreed to spend a summer with him and the children on the Costa del Sol in Spain, two years after our Italian experience.

Renting another villa, we lived with families from all over the world in an international community. Our days were spent mostly at the beach or pool where we met some of our neighbors and socialized a bit. They were friendly and pleasant, and it was interesting to see the differing parenting styles from culture to culture. The boys played lots of board games with Werner, while Susan, our helper Rachel, and I often went to the nearby town of Estepona, where we meandered through the local shops. Werner and I remained distant. The trip was primarily about family.

While at the pool I noticed Werner's attraction to another

woman, which reopened my unhealed wound and the pain of betrayal. I felt threatened, believing it went further than flirtation, but I chose not to confront him. I felt too vulnerable to address that.

On one of my shopping expeditions I bought my first bikini, and I looked and felt great in it. I went braless for a time, beginning to honor and feel the beauty of my body for myself. Werner made no comment on either.

More and more I felt the hopelessness of my marriage, yet I was not prepared to end it. Feeling trapped in my dependency and raw in my hurt and anger, it was agonizing to live in my own skin. My hopes for "happily ever after" were dying. I wished I could just run away from him as fast and as far as possible. Yet how would I cope with life on my own, and how would a separation affect our children?

I resolved to make the best of the time in Spain, try to see it as an adventure and enjoy what it had to offer. Postponing my marital concerns as well as I could, I would deal with next steps when I returned home.

I found Spain very beautiful, although the culture felt heavy, not as free or happy as Italy. Shopkeepers felt more repressed and aloof. This was during Franco's fascist regime, and it was unnerving to pass soldiers armed with bayonets in the streets. But it was wondrous to drive through the countryside, seeing ancient aqueducts and wide expanses of richly colored rolling hills, and wandering through the historic and interesting towns of Segovia and Toledo. We visited the huge Prado Museum in Madrid and viewed the impressive masterpieces of Velasquez, Goya, and El Greco. The children became bored by the docent's longwinded, detailed descriptions, breaking into contagious giggles that were impossible for even me to contain.

We shared many novel and amusing family times. One evening when out for dinner we ordered sangria and allowed the children to taste it, only to find that the bartender had put salt in the pitcher instead of sugar. Never will I forget that taste, or their sour faces after sampling it. We took trips to nearby Marbella to see chic hotels and shops, went to the beaches, and grilled fresh sardines with hot winds blowing in our faces. We watched flamenco dancing with dramatic rhythms, women in sexy red costumes dancing with strong, slender men. We all enjoyed the unique sights, sounds, and tastes of Spain.

As the summer drew to a close, Werner wanted to go to the Munich Olympics. I was not willing to extend my time abroad and anxious to get home and have some separation. Both would comfort me. I wanted to start thinking of ways I might gain the strength and courage I would need if I were to leave him. I was eager to see my therapist to discuss how to move forward, knowing there was a major mountain to climb but with no idea how to do that.

Werner and I agreed that he would take the two older boys to the Olympics, and I would go home with the two younger children. However, a Palestinian group attacked and killed eleven Israeli athletes in Munich, as Werner and the boys were traveling. They never got to the Village and came directly home.

I saw darkness everywhere, in myself, in my marriage, and in the world. The same anti-Semitism in Germany that almost killed Werner when he was a toddler prevented him and my sons from reaching the Munich Olympics thirty-five years later.

Fascism eroded Spain's beauty, while Werner's ongoing interest in other women undermined my belief in my own. I couldn't do anything about fascism or anti-Semitism, but I was determined to do something about myself.

f i f t e e n

GOING DEEPER

FEELING UNSEEN AND LONELY, WITH AN URGENT DESIRE TO
strengthen myself emotionally, I went back to John and asked
for help. He was extremely gentle with me as he said, "Jane, there
is no hurry to leave your marriage. Your primary work is about
yourself, healing the emotional wounds of neglect from your
childhood. You might consider The Path, the spiritual process
I told you about. Think about it and let me know if you want
that. I also suggest that you engage in some creative focus." I left
his office totally confused. My work with John was done. Why
wasn't he suggesting that we continue together?

Living in Rye, New York I was close to Wainwright House, a
prestigious human resource center. I often attended presenta-
tions there, and now that I was at a crossroads, I was particularly
interested in checking out new possibilities. I noticed a program
given by Robert Johnson, a renowned Jungian analyst and author.
I didn't know anything about Jung's work other than that he was
a disciple of Freud in the beginning years of psychiatry.

My decision to attend that program was life changing, as

Robert Johnson introduced his student and protégé, Jan Perkins. Jan was a brilliant, attractive, approachable young man who was locally available for consultations. He spoke clearly and understandably about the meaning and importance of dreams and the gift of interpreting them. I was immediately sold on the idea and contacted him.

It was as though I was being led by the hand to my next teacher. After my conversation with John, I was shown exactly where to go. It wasn't a process of research, but some seeming coincidence that was exactly the place I needed to be.

At the very beginning of our process I told Jan a simple dream. I was in a car with Werner. He was driving, and I was in the passenger seat. That's all there was to it.

An hour later I knew that was the way I was living my life. I was a passenger on Werner's trip, giving him my time, energy, and support while not attending to my own direction. In the many weeks that followed, Jan and I talked about me: my needs, my desires, my interests, what I would like to pursue. I was engaging with my individuality, separate from relationship.

I was excited and interested to be focused on myself, yet it also felt unfamiliar and uncomfortable. Although there was much that didn't please me about being Werner's "passenger," it was less daunting than going through the challenging process of sourcing my own life path. Gratefully I had many distractions, being primarily responsible for four children, as I eased my way into dealing with my own course.

For two and a half years I kept a journal of my dreams, and in each session Jan and I worked together to interpret them. It was fun, like figuring out a puzzle, only these puzzle pieces were of life changing significance.

My marriage and family life continued much as it had been, but I was different. I began to enjoy being me, acknowledging and liking myself and what I was bringing to the party. I was less angry, and Werner's absences became more welcomed. I felt happier and more peaceful, and I was creating that result! My major focus was on taking care of my children and myself.

Feeling encouraged, I was ready for more. I felt ready to start the spiritual process John had talked about, The Path. It was a community led by a woman called "The Guide" who channeled lectures received from a spiritual dimension. It all seemed pretty far out to me, but since I trusted John I was willing. I liked what "The Guide" said and decided to disregard my inner discussion about the source.

There was much to learn about the ego and the soul. She taught how the ego dominates the soul until discovered; after that, the ego is seen simply as a belief system. I could then become the witness to both my ego and soul, and begin to access my soul more frequently. How magnificent it would be to connect with an eternal level of myself.

"The Guide" taught that the ego speaks loudly and the soul speaks in whispers. The ego will continue to dominate until we identify its patterns. While I had never thought about it like that, it made sense to me. I accepted that premise since I wasn't too aware of my soul's voice. In any case, I thought, it would be positive to understand how my ego operates.

I began working with a Path counselor who gave much attention to what she termed my "negativity" in order to correct it. Biweekly ninety-minute sessions were filled with discussions about my negative patterns: self-judgment, difficulty in saying no, an inability to express my wants and to prioritize myself. After several months of doing this I began to feel that I was going downhill, that I *was* my negativity.

Instinctively, I reached for another spiritual process and found Unity Center of New York, led by Eric Butterworth. I have no recollection of how I got there, perhaps something as simple as an ad in the *New York Times*. I went into New York City by train on Tuesdays for noon lectures and returned home in time to pick up my children after school. Since the concepts were new and difficult for me to accept and my resistance was strong, I fell asleep during most talks. Still, I went every available Tuesday.

Although it was challenging to take in what Eric Butterworth was teaching, I wanted to believe it and feel it. He said that Spirit lives in each of us, a life force that we express as individuals every day. He taught that we are intrinsically connected to a formless, loving Energy called God, that we live in a benevolent Universe, connected to everyone and everything. We are never alone or separate despite the definition of our physical bodies. I wanted to believe all of this. For the first time spirituality had relevance for me.

Occasionally I went to his Sunday morning services in Avery Fisher Hall at Lincoln Center, shocked to see thousands of people there. He assured us that, through meditation and personal focus, each individual can harness the creative power of the Universe for the benefit of themselves and others. He talked about love, forgiveness, and joy. It all felt so different from what I had learned as a child in Sunday school.

Coincidentally, the Tuesday noon Unity lectures were held at the same time as my counseling sessions. Since I felt nourished by the talks and wanted to go to them weekly, I asked my counselor to change my session time to allow me to do both. She had no other free time and insisted that I was avoiding my negativity. I knew that was not true. She said that I had to make a choice to meet it or not. Although I did want to continue with her, I was growing in my Unity connection and needed to find some inner balance. She held her position so I left the Path and attended Eric Butterworth's Unity talks weekly. I took a stand for my soul.

I believe that coincidences are Universal gifts rather than haphazard events. Perhaps I had already gained what I needed from my Path sessions. The ability to differentiate between my ego and soul was enormously powerful.

In my short time in The Path I learned that my happiness depended on me, not on others. I learned how automatic it was for me to prioritize others' wants, and how difficult it was for me to act on my own behalf. I learned that my yes was often not authentic, not a yes at all but an unwillingness to risk saying no. I judged myself for not being authentic and for being weak. I learned that I was angry with others for getting what they wanted while I didn't. This awareness guided me to make happier, more loving decisions. I could now give some of my love to myself.

Eric Butterworth spoke about connecting our spiritual feelings to our innate talents, allowing them to inspire us. John had also encouraged my creative expression. I thought about enjoyable childhood experiences, singing with my Dad and being part of a small chorus in the music school where I took cello lessons. I remembered singing the Lord's Prayer, how beautiful the harmonies were, and decided to join a performance singing class.

The classes were great fun, an opportunity to be authentic, to stretch myself and be seen. As I slowly gained confidence, I began to express myself emotionally through song. I sang love songs, "For Once in My Life," sexy songs, "Peel Me a Grape," vulnerable songs, "I Want to Be a Lion Tamer"—a song about being noticed. It was a different feeling, deeper than emotion, coming from a more rooted place. It felt good to realize that my soul journey didn't need to be a heavy trip.

My singing class was a bonded and supportive community. We became good friends. Classmates appreciated the risk of performing and honored each singer's talents, efforts, and courage. After two years Ron, one of the young men in the class, asked me about my marriage, saying that he often felt sadness in my music. I hadn't realized I was that transparent.

This was a rich time of exploring my conscious and unconscious mind, my spirituality and creativity. I felt expanded, hopeful and inspired, happy to include myself in my focus.

With all these positives, it was more urgent than ever that I deal with my marriage. It was too much like my unhappy childhood home where I received little attention, support or acknowledgment. I had learned that I am more than the accommodating, self-denying roles I had been playing. I had come far enough to see that they were not authentic, and I didn't want to spend the rest of my life continuing to act them out. I wanted to be happy, discovering and sharing my talents while being loving to myself and others.

Step by step, my inner work was leading me there, like breaths of fresh air giving me energy and hope. I would keep going, no matter what.

sixteen

MY GUIDES

ERIC BUTTERWORTH TAUGHT THAT MEDITATION IS AN INDI-
vidual's direct gateway to their soul and the Universe. I wanted to
have that experience and decided to begin a meditation practice.

I contacted a teacher who gave me poems to read before sitting in silence. Daily I sat in the sauna that Werner had designed,
a small, quiet, candle-lit, cedar-scented space. I found the discipline surprisingly comforting and peaceful, a time to do nothing
in an otherwise hectic existence. Listening to my mind chatter
allowed me to hear the frenetic constancy of it, making it less
trustworthy than I once believed it was. Depending on the day,
I was happy or sad, angry or afraid. Up and down, my feelings
were in response to my thoughts or outer events. Meditation
gave me a window into my deeper self, which I could feel only
when my mind and emotions were still.

I looked forward to that time every day. After some months I
began to pose questions about my marriage and family, speaking
them aloud into the silence. It felt good to state my concerns and
let them go, rather than trying to figure everything out. After a

while, I began to hear voiceless messages that I found scary. At times I thought I was going off the deep end by giving power to an invisible voice, yet something inside urged me to trust. The messages always came through in the most loving and clear way, challenging when needed, yet with such grace that I took them in easily.

Although the source of these messages was a mystery, my meditation teacher assured me that some people receive visual images and others hear or feel guidance. The thoughts I heard were simple and nourishing: "Jane, slow down and rest." or "Sometimes it is wise to say no." I was receiving enlightened, comforting support and direction that added to my insight and spiritual awareness. It was all new and profound, although it often felt risky.

In time I decided that the messages came from my spiritual Guides, and after several months I began to pose personal questions to them. Their answers were delivered in calm, measured words, with extraordinary compassion and brilliance.

How can I explain more about my Guides? I love them so. They have been my teachers, my supporters, my encouragers, my vision, my admirers, my challengers, my dearest friends. Invisible as they are, they are very real to me. They speak to me as soon as I am quiet enough to listen. They answer my questions, or when I simply ask them to tell me what they see as most pressing, they address what I have been unwilling to see.

I don't know if they are entities outside of me, or a part of my most evolved mind, perhaps my highly developed intuition. I don't know whether they are one or several. Yet their language is different from my everyday speaking, so I have chosen to believe they are angels surrounding me to lead me higher.

When I ask what lies underneath my unhappiness or uncertainty, I receive clear insight and suggestions. When I succeed, I receive acknowledgment and praise. When I am hard on myself,

I receive gentle reminders about self-care. When I reach toward them in gratitude, I receive their sweet love.

Meditation became the high point of my day. My Guides' messages were always relevant and beautiful. Since I wanted to remember the messages forever, I bought a decorative journal to record them. Surprisingly I found it easy to do that. It was as though each word was deeply etched in my mind. I was able to transcribe the communications, word by word, to recall whenever I desired. I did this daily and collected scores of powerful passages, a practice I continue to this day.

No matter what my Guides have said, whether soothing or challenging, I have listened and surrendered to them. I have invited them to change my life. It gives me great peace to put my faith in a source beyond my intellect, for my Guides see deeper and wider than I can on my own. They offer a map to follow, with support each step of the way. Sharing whatever is to be addressed here and now, I ask, I receive, I digest and when ready, I act. My more than forty years of guidance has never, ever led me anywhere but in the most beneficial direction.

I have learned to accept the power of the immaterial, whether guidance from other entities, my higher self, or teachers who are more evolved than I am. It doesn't matter. What does matter is that I am becoming a more faith-filled person, more able to allow, follow, and trust what I cannot yet see. And though I was still in the early stages of my relationship with my Guides as I sat with them in the cedar-scented sauna, I trusted them implicitly. As time went on I heard more extensive answers and instruction. Sometimes their ideas felt like lightning bolts shocking my world, yet they were always delivered with the quietest, kindest, most loving energy. One day I heard: "You are now ready. It is time to leave your marriage."

It felt like graduation day, cause for celebration but with the sorrow of leaving dreams behind as well as the apprehension of being cast into an unknown void. Thankfully there was always a generous time gap between receiving a message and taking action, while the guidance gently worked within me to finally accept and embrace.

s e v e n t e e n

PUPPIES

AS MY GUIDES CALMLY MOVED ME TO A PLACE OF BEING ABLE to let go of my marriage, time was moving me closer to another stage of letting go. My children were growing, maturing into their individual selves more each day. I had to grow into acceptance of what felt like loss, and I found an unexpected guide was leading the way.

Our family's dog Lizzie, an adorable silver Yorkshire terrier, had a litter of four puppies. She was totally devoted to them, nursed them, licked them clean, and watched over them with great devotion for six weeks. Suddenly she pushed them away from feeding and nuzzling, growling at them as they struggled to connect. I was upset. Since I had never been around a dog giving birth, I called my vet to find out what was wrong. The vet said that Lizzie's behavior was normal and that it was time for the puppies to separate from her. This was so different from my ideas of mothering that I began to wonder if she innately knew something that I needed to accept. Sad as we would be to part with the puppies, it was time to start thinking about letting them go.

This all started when my seven-year-old son Barry came home from his friend Greg's house having fallen in love with his Yorkie. He asked if he could have one. I, in my busyness, put him off by telling him he could when he was ten. He didn't argue with my decision, which was unusual, and I never gave it another thought until he approached me on his tenth birthday: "Can I have it now?" I said, "Have what? He answered: "The Yorkie you promised I could have when I was ten."

I was stunned at my own insensitivity, and that Barry would have held that promise in his mind for three years without ever saying anything! There was no turning back from that promise. I had never had a dog as a child and had no idea what it would be like. To me it was just another being to take care of, and I had my plate full with four kids, an often absent husband, and my own activities.

All four children and Werner were thrilled about the prospect of having a dog. We located a Yorkshire terrier breeder in upstate New York who had several puppies. If you have ever seen a Yorkie puppy, you know that they are simply irresistible, like live stuffed animals. A frisky one came running toward Barry and rolled over on his back with his legs in the air, asking to be petted. Of course he was the one Barry chose, and we took him home. The children were excited, naming him Clyde after a star New York Knicks basketball player. In no time, each of us became very attached to him.

One year later, the children were asking for another puppy and I, smitten with Clyde, agreed. We bought another Yorkie, this time a female, and decided to call her Lizzie, short for Queen Elizabeth of Greenhaven, the name of our community. She was larger and not the perfect specimen Clyde was, but she was feisty, quirky, playful and, most of all, very independent. Rather than stately, she was funny, often cocking her head, thinking about whether to obey a command or decide against it, usually opting for the latter.

Almost a year later Lizzie had a litter of four puppies. She gave birth to them in an upstairs closet and guarded the room fiercely. Anytime a visitor came, she ran upstairs to protect the door. She would not permit anyone in that room except family members.

One day she woke up and that was that, no more feeding. She was done, and we knew it was our time to take over. I put the four puppies in a playpen and gave them cereal as the vet advised. Lizzie checked on them and played with them from time to time during the day, but with far less involvement; yet they thrived and were happy and healthy.

Two weeks later it became necessary to tell the children that we could not have six dogs in our household. We needed to find homes for the puppies. They were distraught and begged to keep just one of them. I agreed, finding it as hard as they did to part with them. They chose the smallest of the litter, a precious fluff, and named him Schultzie after a character on *Hogan's Heroes*.

Werner had a friend who was excited to take one of the puppies. That was a great relief to me, knowing that she would be kind and caring. She came to our house directly after work wearing a suit, chose the prettiest of the four, slipped him under her jacket lapel and quickly left.

Within seconds Lizzie started to tear around the house looking for her puppy. For hours she ran up the stairs, down the stairs, from the front of the house to the back, searching every room, every closet that was open, under every piece of furniture, frantically looking for him. I tried to pick her up but there was no stopping her from her search. Up and down, round and round, faster and faster. Finally she stopped and lay down, exhausted.

I said my goodnights to the children and spent the whole night lying on the floor stroking her. Hour after hour passed. She just lay quietly, staring into space while I stroked her. I was sad for Lizzie's loss and my own yet knew it was a necessary step. Her puppy needed to have a permanent home, and she needed to separate from him.

Hours later it dawned on me that my children did not belong to me either. Letting go of them would be far more gradual, giving me years to gently reduce my involvement. Yet I was more aware than ever that each had his or her own destiny and would leave me in the years ahead.

I was relieved to be reminded that their lives did not depend solely on me. Many other people and situations would impact them. More aware of my separateness, I encouraged each child to make his or her own choices, to become as independent as possible. I would be certain to support them. Eventually the time would come for me to let them go and find their place in the world. Perhaps I would even need to nudge them out the door.

I never forgot the pain I felt for Lizzie's loss that night, pain that I might someday feel. Nor did I forget that my children had their own paths to follow, and I would increasingly allow them to lead their way.

eighteen

DIVORCE

DIVORCE WAS THE DEFINING MOMENT OF MY ADULT LIFE, A line in the sand proclaiming my willingness to stand in my soul despite all the risks and my fears. It was far from a practical decision. I had no career, and I had concerns about negotiating a fair settlement with Werner. Yet for me, divorce was a matter of psychological and spiritual life or death. I chose life, knowing that I also would face huge challenges.

Five years after beginning my inner journey, I had gained sufficient insight and strength to see that it was impossible for Werner to meet my desires, needs, and values. At the time I married I did not intimately know him or myself. He was a replication of my past. My marriage mirrored the inattentiveness I experienced with Mom, repeated the bargain I made with Walt whom I served in exchange for access to the world, and embodied what Dad thought would provide a secure and happy life. I could not have made the decision to leave were it not for the hundreds of hours I had spent in groups, private therapy sessions, classes, meditation, and trainings.

I could no longer accept being minimized in my marriage. I wanted emotional and sensual intimacy, but what I had was distance and disloyalty. I wanted to feel loved and loving, yet I felt dishonored and angry. Even with no map to follow, I was willing to navigate the vastness of the unknown to create the life I envisioned.

Werner was a restless man, attractive, intelligent, articulate, creative, enterprising, and interesting. Through time I found that he was also self-centered, competitive, and extremely limited in his emotional capacity. Often thoughtless and irresponsible, he frequently felt victimized by his co-workers, his parents, and me. While he was an excellent provider, he was not yielding or tender. He was a great networker who knew many people, yet he had no close friends.

Werner grew up in a male-dominated German family in which control and competition were the norm. He ignored or diminished my strengths, attempting to establish superiority while hiding from his weaknesses. Even though I admired his abilities, I found that I frequently didn't like him.

My desire for partnership and intimacy had long been frustrated by Werner's personal and business priorities. I could not accept his neglect and disloyalty, nor could I accept his allegiance to his career success as the key to his value and identity. While I loved being my children's Mom, I became increasingly lonely as Werner's thoughtless choices continued. My marriage was empty. Soon after retirement, he turned to acting and singing classes that replaced business as his priority. My dream that closeness would come when his work required less energy was shattered.

Still I was not ready to leave, unprepared to live my life without the structure of marriage. I was financially and emotionally dependent and saw the integrity of the family unit as more important than my personal happiness. I judged myself as selfish for even considering throwing five other lives into turmoil.

I was worried about the impact on the children and how they would fare, but I was also worried about the unhealthy model of marriage they were internalizing. The more I saw that the quality of my life seemed of little concern to Werner, the more I wanted out.

What work would I do? Could I do? How would I earn enough money to manage? I didn't want to teach again, having my daily work be with children while I had four more at home. Who could I ask for help? How decent would Werner be in the financial settlement? How reliable would he be in keeping it? How would it feel to give up the affluent lifestyle I had become so used to and enjoyed? How would it be to live on my own? Day after day these scary questions raced through my mind. Yet how could I live with myself, never giving myself the chance to flourish, feel happy and whole, to stand tall?

Tension was growing between us. In one of our last disagreements, incredibly and without warning, Werner threw my meditation journal into the fireplace. Had he read it, or did he intuit my intention to follow the guidance in it? I stood horrified and immobilized, watching my treasured book slowly disintegrate into ash. I couldn't speak. A deep breach had taken place. Every one of my Guides' communications was burning. Werner didn't realize that the essence of each message would remain in my mind forever.

Weeks later we attended Werner's Uncle Julius' funeral. Julius was a sweet and timid man I hardly knew. Yet as the rabbi spoke I began to cry. Family members exchanged perplexed glances with each other about my disproportionate response. I was as dumbfounded as they were until I realized that I was mourning the death of my marriage.

We had attended some couples groups that made little difference. In my individual therapy I became aware of and expressed my thoughts, feelings, wants, needs and vision, building necessary inner resources. My Guides' messages had greatly strengthened me, giving me the courage to take action. They told me that there is not only physical death but also psychological and spiritual death. Feeling renewed faith, I decided to take the leap and leave my marriage.

At age thirty-nine, with no job or money of my own, and four children ages seventeen, fourteen, twelve, and ten, I told Werner our marriage was over. He was shocked, never believing that could happen. It was an ugly scene. As is true for many people when they are threatened, he became angry, forceful and intimidating.

I was doing laundry in the basement of our home, frightened yet steadfast in my decision. I walked up the steep, narrow basement stairs, my arms filled with neatly folded towels piled high resting under my chin. He stood at the top blocking the doorway, arms outstretched to the doorframe and said, "You are almost forty years old with four children, no job, and no money. You'll never be able to do this."

I could feel the fury rising from my depths. I continued walking up the stairs, flung his arm away from the doorway and said, "Watch me!" Using anger as my fuel, I began my steps toward building a new life.

From that stance I instituted a divorce process. Along with intense anger and fear, I had a deep longing to feel whole: womanly, sensual, loving and loved. I saw my choice as self-love or pain and anger, life as an adult or a subordinate wife mothering four children and a dependent husband. That is what I was and that is what he wanted.

Shortly after I announced my intention to split, Werner called to ask if I would pick him up at the Mercedes repair shop. I agreed, and as I exited the highway, I saw him in his bright blue parka walking along the side of the road. Why didn't he wait at the repair shop? Perhaps he was too upset to contain himself there.

I slowed down and saw a man who looked like a lost child. His hood was tied tightly around his face with no hairline showing, nose running, and tears streaming down his cheeks, appearing abandoned and devastated. It was a most shocking contrast to his typical in-charge demeanor.

The day he moved out of our home was traumatic. I was in the kitchen; Werner was upstairs in the master bedroom packing. I heard a loud noise, then gut-wrenching wails. Running upstairs I saw that he had ripped the pole out of the closet. It had snapped, leaving his clothes in a heap on the floor. I looked into his eyes and saw an old man, unfocused and confused. Frightened, I left the room to compose myself. He walked downstairs after me, into the hallway, shuffling his feet. As he entered the kitchen, his usually sparkling eyes still glazed, he asked me if he was walking like an old man, like his Uncle Eugene. I said yes. He didn't answer, turned around and shuffled down the hall and up the stairs. I followed to help him pack and was relieved when he finally left with his belongings.

I have never understood what happened to him that day. I always saw Werner as so sure of himself that the emotional state I witnessed still disturbs me.

Having no control over my decision to separate, Werner became vengeful. Using money and time as weapons, he was retaliatory and punishing, offering a settlement that was overwhelmingly in his favor.

Although I thought we were a wealthy family, in actuality he was a wealthy man. His offer was that our four children and I were to live on less than a third of what our family of six had been spending. Since settlements were based on averaging the past five years earnings and Werner had been retired for three of those years, his earning capacity was greatly distorted and diluted. He said he would supply more only "if able."

I saw these terms as inadequate and unjust, and that I would not have the means to support us or maintain the family home. Yet I would not allow the prospect of years of hostile court battles to deplete me and distract me from raising our children and creating my necessary career path. My purpose in choosing this divorce was to create a happy life.

Seeing that he was unwavering in his position, I agreed to his terms. I accepted the house as my capital settlement to ensure continuity. I feared that the children and I would have to move if I didn't keep the house. I was not prepared to take that risk, believing that moving in addition to the divorce would be destructive for the children and a major hardship for me.

Werner did not include all four children in his visits except for rare vacations to distant places. This left me with continual daily parenting responsibility for eight more years, as one by one each child went off to college. His unwillingness to take responsibility for his contribution to the collapse of our marriage, and his continual punishing choices during the year between our separation agreement and divorce, confirmed my decision to dissolve the marriage.

I wanted to remember that he had contributed extraordinary positives to my life: four beloved children, the security of a family structure, financial affluence, and opportunities to travel the world. I realized later that our marriage spared me from being alone, a deep-seated fear I held until I was ready to confront it. In exploring the roots of his own unhappiness, Werner led me to the first steps of my inner journey. Ironically, that eventually freed me to leave him, and it also became the passion of my adult life.

Divorces increased at that time, as large numbers of women decided to grow up and take on the full responsibilities of adulthood. Being single parents added to our responsibilities and compromised our freedom. My children were both a strong support and a challenge. They were grounding rods and daily motivations to stay sane and focused, but they were angry and sad about the separation and sometimes acted out. Many a morning when it was difficult to face the day, they reminded me that life goes on, homework needs to be completed, breakfast needs to be prepared, and book bags need to be packed. My attention was required.

My loyal handyman Frank, who took care of our house for over twelve years, stopped by every morning to be sure I was up and into my day. He came in the kitchen door and called upstairs: "Missy, I'm setting up the coffee." We sat and chatted about family, how my kids were doing and neighborhood news. Frank had a wife and two adult children he sent through college by prospering in his one-man business. He adored his daughter but was disappointed that his son, who became a high-level executive in a large accounting firm, didn't have time for him.

I had always felt Frank's fondness for our family as he watched the kids grow up, yet I was surprised and moved by his love and devotion to me. He was my good friend, and while I felt his attraction to me as a woman, he never crossed that line. Each morning he stayed until he saw that I was settled once the children left for school.

I was always happy to see Frank's worn black truck turn into my driveway. He did whatever was needed to keep the house in good repair. Now and then he would send a minimal bill giving the appearance that I was compensating him. He wanted to be my hero, and he was.

Months later he told me he needed a new truck but that it was too expensive. He thought he was too old to make that investment and seemed very sad, saying that he would soon have to give up his business. He had gone to the local park to check if they needed a handyman on staff but was turned down. Instead, they offered him a job at the ticket booth greeting visitors. He tried that for one day and quit.

Frank didn't show up the next morning, or the next. I called his home and learned that he had died peacefully in his sleep two nights before. I was heartbroken. He was my port in stormy waters, my godsend. His loving attention and support was my daily nourishment. I learned that sometimes love comes from the most unlikely source.

The hardships of divorce were formidable, yet they were also expansive. I found that I was stronger and more resourceful than I'd ever imagined. I appreciated the peaceful and pleasurable moments I created, knowing what made me feel good. I valued the simplicity of my life, its order and purpose.

I learned that I count, that my happiness counts, and that while I was pleased to serve others, doing so would never again be at my expense. I had always longed to be seen and appreciated, and I was now giving myself that attention. I found people who supported me. I felt comforted to be in contact with my inner guidance, trusting that I would find a new creative expression that would be my work in the world.

I also learned about money, what it provides and what it doesn't. I didn't miss the frills as much as I realized the necessity of creating financial security.

My greatest appreciation was in reclaiming my individuality. I was now a fully responsible grown-up making my own decisions and forging my own way, an adult woman facing my challenges and welcoming the rewards of meeting them. Even with all the hardships and unknowns, I acknowledged that I was brave enough to give myself a chance for a happy life.

nineteen

STAYING HOME

LIFE BECAME SIMPLE. THERE WAS NOTHING TO DO BUT STAY home and take care of my children, the house, and myself. There was no money for anything except essentials: food, house, car, medical needs, children's clothing, and taxes. I was surprised that to the degree my life choices were reduced, my internal focus became sharper. I was far more aware of my moment-to-moment thoughts, feelings, and bodily sensations. It was an intense time, yet I was calm. Werner's absence revealed the enormous strain his presence had caused. I felt safer on my own, knowing that I was able to keep myself in balance and my responsibilities in order.

Not knowing where to turn for work, I asked for direction in my daily meditation. The repeated guidance I received was that the most important thing was for me to stay home, be a consistent presence, take care of my children, and do daily meditation practice. While I couldn't see how that would solve my concerns, I followed that guidance diligently.

A friend introduced me to Abraham, a spiritual channel that

teaches the Law of Attraction. In essence, that law says that we draw to ourselves whatever we focus on, wanted or not, and that our outer experience always matches our mental-emotional vibration. When I envision experiences I want, I feel happy and peaceful. When I imagine things I don't want, I feel sad, scared, or mad. I found that teaching to be simple, interesting and helpful, and I began to consciously focus more on the peaceful life I was living, envisioning the specifics of the happy life I could have.

Sometimes that was challenging to do as house maintenance issues began to show up. The icemaker was the first casualty of our new lifestyle. The children were extremely put out by that. Then came major repairs: furnace breakdowns and needing to replace supporting beams in the basement. To make matters worse, escalating inflation had become a national economic problem. Oil became scarce and prices skyrocketed. There were long lines at gas stations; people were often turned away when the pumps ran dry. I was particularly fortunate that the owner of my local gas station offered to fill my tank whenever I needed. He suggested that I park my car in the adjacent lot and he would take care of it. I was so grateful!

The high costs of heating oil and repairs were making it impossible to maintain the house within my means. At the same time, mortgage rates soared to double digits, making a sale hopeless. Financial pressures had become severe and were mounting. My supportive banker Marie suggested that I open a line of credit and she helped me do that.

I completely stopped spending any money on myself and mentally calculated the cost of items in my supermarket cart before checkout. The first year I managed to be only $2,000 over my drastically reduced budget. My brother surprised me with a check for $3,000 with a note that read: "In case the roof is leaking." The second year I managed to keep living costs within my plan but needed money for taxes. I asked my Mom for help, which she gave me, but said that she couldn't spare more since her funds were invested. I lived with that high level of financial stress for five years; my greatest concern was not knowing when and how I would resolve the shortfall.

When the children were with their Dad, he treated them to the events and experiences they were accustomed to. I never told them of the magnitude of my financial shift so they were completely unaware of the stress that caused. I found it difficult to listen graciously as they told me about the movies, shows, sporting events, restaurants, and vacation plans that filled their visits. I felt hurt and angry that I was the only family member whose financial life had suffered and ashamed that I was jealous of my children's pleasure.

During this time, my Guides continued to suggest that I stay home, be a consistent presence, take care of my children, and do daily meditation practice.

My back-up plan, in case I heard no feasible idea in meditation, was to ask well-placed friends for help in finding a job. I didn't want to commute to New York City and be unavailable to my children, didn't want a full-time job, and was not drawn to business. I needed to forge a career path that earned sufficient income and that served my interests. While feeling scared, I was also somewhat hopeful that a new start would be interesting and perhaps open the door to what I was meant to do, whatever that was. If I could just supplement what I received from Werner, I trusted that, in time, I would grow in my purpose and create income through the work I chose.

While the children seemed to adjust fairly well to their new home life, they certainly were affected. Bill was angry, happy to be going away to college. Dick was sad and withdrawn, and Barry was acting out in school. Susan did well. None of them liked being asked to help in the kitchen and clean their rooms, nor did they talk much about their visits with Werner. I believe those visits were more difficult for Susan. Sometimes she asked me to go with her when she was to see Werner alone, which I did several times.

Connection to myself, my children, and friends filled me. I don't know what I would have done without the love of friends: Joan, Elin, and Ron. My cousin Joan, who had been divorced for years and understood what I was going through, was a great support. We grew up together and were close as little girls when we played with our dolls. We spoke on the phone every night after my children went to bed. She encouraged me and was always there to offer a laugh. Laughter helped a lot.

I was always welcome at Elin's home. That felt like old times. Our bond of raising our babies together was strong, and she was as warm and generous as ever, offering me treats that I was used to and could no longer afford. I always felt taken care of in her home, and we visited in the afternoons while our children were in school and Bob was at work.

Ron, my young friend from singing class, called after I had not shown up for a couple of weeks. "How are you? Are you OK? We miss you!"

I answered: "Big changes are going on. I told Werner that I wanted a divorce. It was an ugly scene. I won't be coming to class since I don't have the freedom or funds to continue."

Ron was not surprised. He said, "Sounds like a tough time. Can I help in any way?" I thanked him and said I would let him know.

Ron called often and became a frequent visitor. He worked at night and was available to visit some afternoons. Although intelligent, he was not well educated, which limited his career options. He was very different from Werner, generous and caring, graciously listening to and supporting me as I shared concerns about my children, career, and money. He helped with the housework, often cooked meals, walked the dogs, and shoveled the snow. I so appreciated his presence at this time of transition.

It wasn't long before our relationship became sexual. Experienced and tender, Ron's comfort and relaxation led me to my own, and to new and deep experiences of pleasure. I grew to delight in and appreciate the joy my body could bring me in a way I had never known. It was a revelation! I felt more alive and beautiful than ever before. When I introduced Ron to my brother, Walt called within hours and angrily asked what I was doing with this "stud." Actually, I was healing the sexual shame of my adolescence.

After the children went to bed and my nightly call with Joan, I exercised. Dancing to Jane Fonda videos many nights a week kept my body looking beautiful and my energy high. My simple life was in sharp contrast to the luxury and special travels I had enjoyed, yet I was happier. I felt more peaceful and had no regrets. My emotional needs were satisfied, my sexual longings finally fulfilled, and my daily life more content. Not feeling the constant strain of dealing with a high-maintenance, untrustworthy, and chaotic man far outweighed the benefits of financial security and a high-end lifestyle. I found myself more relaxed, even with insufficient money and challenging children, than I had been in my marriage where I always needed to be super-vigilant, never knowing what neglect or drama was coming next.

I was more focused and hoped that as my life became fuller, I would be able to maintain this level of clarity about what was important to me and made me happy. I promised myself that I would continue to address any uncomfortable feelings that came up to keep myself emotionally honest. Despite the challenges I was facing, I felt better. I was taking care of myself, doing what I needed to do, and grateful that I had taken this giant step.

t w e n t y

NABEL'S NURSERY

ONE DAY DURING MEDITATION, A YEAR AFTER WERNER MOVED out, I received guidance to get a temporary job in a plant nursery. That seemed unusual to me but I had learned to listen to my Guides since they always led me to something valuable.

For many years I had purchased my plants and flowers from a local nursery and, interested in learning about them, had gotten to know Rudy, the owner, quite well. Each spring I had bought large amounts of different varieties of beautiful flowers to fill our front and back yards to overflowing.

Rudy was quite surprised when, in the gray cold of January, I drove up to his nursery in my old Mercedes and asked him for a job. He scoffed at the idea, telling me it was hard work and that he paid his employees $3.00 an hour. He said, "This is not the job for you. It is physically demanding. I hire kids to do the seasonal work, getting ready for spring sales. They start in late February, and I lay them off after July Fourth."

That timeframe sounded perfect for me as my children were in school until late June. I told him I wanted the job, but he still said, "It's not for you." I asked him for the names of his competitors so I could inquire elsewhere. He gladly gave me the names of the two he knew best.

I went to each of them and both turned me down. I am not sure why, but my guess is that I didn't look like I fit the job description. Returning to Rudy, I again asked to work there. This time he said, "You are really serious, aren't you?" I told him I was, and he offered me the job.

Having no idea why I was doing this, other than trusting my guidance, I began work near the end of February. My workmates were women half my age, yet we got along well and had nice times together.

Our first task was to plant six rows of seeds lengthwise in 18" x 24" boxes, labeling each one. Hour after hour we planted tiny seeds into countless boxes. After planting we carefully fed them with small amounts of water. The process required very little thought and was quite meditative. We had some pleasant conversations and frequent long, comfortable silences.

Weeks later the seeds began to germinate, sprouting from the soil as fragile, delicate, silk-like threads. We carefully transplanted each shoot into a compartment of a plastic six-pack, where each "pot" was 1½" square. There were hundreds and hundreds of these six-packs. Small varieties remained in the six-pack, but all those that would become larger had to again be transplanted into 4" pots months later.

The task of transplanting went on through March. Day after day there were more plants to move from six-packs to pots, water, and place in one of the seven greenhouses. By this time, small leaves and buds were showing, growing closer to the mature appearance they would eventually have. I found myself interested in their differences and enjoyed tending them, watching them mature into themselves. It was as if they were developing from fetuses to infants to beautiful children.

By the end of March all seven greenhouses were filled with pots of flowers. The owner purchased many larger varieties from other suppliers: hanging baskets of fuchsia, hibiscus, impatiens, begonias, and salvia, spreading color through the greenhouses. Days were easy and quiet, with much less to do. Just the few of us worked daily in the nursery, peacefully watering thousands of gorgeous flowers.

By April the nursery felt like a wonderland. It was a delight to see new flowers profusely popping by the hour and showing off everywhere. Beautiful and plentiful, they were a balm to my senses. Reds, whites, yellows, oranges, blues, purples, greens, all in varying shades of intensity. The space was now miraculously filled with them, a sharp contrast to the vacant, cold, bare structures I saw in the darkness of winter. I began to understand why my Guides suggested this experience. Bringing me back to nature gave me a tranquil place to be, using my energy to nurture growth while being nourished in return.

Mother's Day weekend came. Beginning at 8:00 on Saturday morning, dozens of cars poured into the parking lot. By noon there were no parking spaces left, and long lines waited in the driveway. People crowded the aisles asking many questions, trying to decide what would be most beautiful for their gardens. Most were considerate and gentle, but some were aggressive and demanding. Hour after hour, the cars arrived empty and left filled with plants and flowers. By the end of the day the greenhouses felt picked over, like they had been pirated. By Sunday evening large, vacant spaces of bare concrete were visible where gorgeous flowers had been just two days before. Every weekend was like that through the Fourth of July. Life at the nursery was busy, fast, noisy and hectic. Plants and flowers were stored in trunks and backseats with tall ones poking through open sunroofs. I felt sad. The owner was delighted.

I thought about my guidance. What was this experience all

about? The nursery was an exquisite blueprint of the life cycle fast-forwarded. My Guides had directed me to quickly experience its creative stages: inception, gestation, birth, fragile early development, joy-filled nurturance, and robust and beautiful maturity. Then letting go. As if watching an animated film, I saw the stages of life unfold within four months.

My job at the nursery was a wise model for life and parenting. Just as Lizzie knew with her puppies, the time comes to let go. We all have to let go even though it is hard. With all the care I gave these plants, they now had their own place in the world. They graced my life for a short time while I fed theirs. Though I did not yet recognize it, this experience was a source of wisdom that I would use in my future career.

When the job ended, I invited my four children to dinner in a fine local Italian restaurant. I had saved three of my $97.50 weekly take-home paychecks for this event, wanting to celebrate my step toward independence. It was the first time we would be out together as a family without their Dad, and I was proud to be hosting them with money I had earned. My children had no idea how much it meant to me to provide this meal. They seemed relaxed and happy, chattering away, by now used to being with each of us separately.

While they enjoyed the dinner, my mind was in the past. As I sat at the head of the oblong table with an empty seat facing me, I felt heartbroken. It was strange how much of my attention that empty space occupied. While I was on my way to creating a new version of myself, in those moments I profoundly felt the cost of my divorce. Although I no longer had to deal with the pain of living with Werner, there was heartbreak, long-lasting heartbreak. I was mourning the death of my broken family structure.

After we got home and the children went to bed I thought about my pain. I recalled my Guides' message that we go through many deaths in life before our physical bodies pass. I remembered sitting with Lizzie the night her first puppy was taken from our home. I thought about how it felt on Mother's Day weekend at Nabel's as the plants I had nurtured daily for four months flew off the shelves. I felt the grief of ending my marriage after giving so much energy and attention to what was now just a memory.

Although I felt heartbroken, I was growing, even though I didn't know what direction my life would take. We prune plants so that they can be healthier and more beautiful; I was doing the same by simplifying my life—meditating, running the house, taking care of my children, and staying open to guidance. A new, unfamiliar, and happier expression of myself was emerging. I trusted that with desire and patience I would create satisfying new beginnings.

twenty one

WORK IN THE WORLD

I CONTINUED TO MEDITATE, RECEIVING LIFE-ALTERING GUID-
ance. One day I heard, "Your work is to be a Family Counselor
specializing in Parent Education, a new concept for which you are
highly qualified. We will support you in creating a curriculum."

I was surprised and excited. The foundation of my Guides'
instruction was that parental modeling is far more influential
than words. Children learn primarily from their parents' attitudes, feelings, and actions. When parents' words are not in line
with their behavior or emotions, children, who are highly receptive, are disturbed and confused. Also, by exercising excessive
control and having limited listening skills, parents often restrict
their children from growing beyond them. All these themes resonated deeply with me.

I had never heard of Parent Education, and it was the first
time I heard the word "parenting." It seemed natural and fitting
for me to do this. I had learned much academically, experientially,
and from my extensive therapy to support this work. My immediate task was to meditate, listen, and record the information I

would be receiving. I did that religiously. I wanted to give this idea a try. It was work I could value, where I believed I would succeed in providing an important service.

In 1976 the only people I knew who focused on parents were Benjamin Spock, Haim Ginott, and Thomas Gordon. All wrote "how to" books. I decided not to study their books immediately, wanting what I was about to create to be fresh and new. I was greatly touched by Kahlil Gibran's book, *The Prophet*, published in 1927. In that group of exquisite poems is an inspiring piece called "On Children":

Your children are not your children.

They are the sons and daughters of Life's longing for itself.

They come through you but not from you.

And though they are with you, yet they belong not to you.

You may strive to be like them

but seek not to make them like you.

For life goes not backward nor tarries with yesterday.

You are the bows from which your children as living arrows

are sent forth.

Gibran's ideas inspired me in creating my Parents School. I enthusiastically continued to meditate and received ideas about curriculum structure, and how and where to present it. This was to be a personal development seminar geared to parents of young children, who would be the most receptive audience, having the greatest desire to give their children their best.

I was guided to offer the course as a public service and approached elementary schools and hospital maternity wards, but neither was interested. My next outreach was to my hometown library, where the Children's Room librarian was the mother of one of my son's friends. She was excited about my idea and sponsored three sessions. She also planned a story time so that children would be happily entertained while their mothers attended the programs.

Although this was the first time I was presenting material to an adult group, it felt easy and natural to me. The series was well received and acknowledged as effective, innovative, and thought provoking. I was invited to return. With the help of the librarian's strong recommendation I was able to interest nearby libraries in hosting my seminars. I also created new programs. When some mothers expressed interest in learning more, I started the Parents School, holding private classes in my home. My counseling practice was born!

I enjoyed presenting the material, interacting with participants, and sharing my knowledge and personal experiences. I was surprised and interested to hear my Guides offering me new thoughts. Their questions and reminders enriched what I was presenting and focused my leadership even more. They gave me ideas like: "Discipline is an important topic; self-discipline is even more important." "How consistent are your decisions?" "How playful are you in your parenting?"

An unexpected pleasure and benefit of my Parents School classes was the creation of a women's network through which we called upon one another for help, support, and friendship outside of our meetings. The participants often told me about their ongoing connection and how our work was creating a community.

Individual and marital issues surfaced in my parenting classes, giving rise to a women's personal development group that I led for fifteen years. We became a close circle, dealing with raising our children; going through divorce, marriage and career changes; and dealing with aging parents and their role as grandparents. Eventually one of our members developed a fatal illness, and we shared the experience of deep grieving. We treasured our connection that brought us solace and strength. I learned that being part of a women's community makes life deeper, richer, and happier.

Participants in both my Parents School classes and personal development group asked for private sessions. I worked with individuals and couples as together we addressed concerns about parenting, marriage, career, addiction, illness, and loss. I connected with them heart to heart and mind to mind, asking questions that kept them focused on what they wanted. We explored what stood in the way of realizing their desires along with their ability and willingness to take next steps.

One day I was surprised to receive an excited phone call from Werner. He had just completed the EST Training, saying, "Jane, you've got to do this. It is fantastic. The change that I feel in myself and heard from hundreds of participants is awesome. I want you to do it. Accept it as my gift to you." I could feel his enthusiasm and sincere desire for me to do EST, perhaps to reconsider the divorce. Although I definitely didn't want any personal relationship with Werner, I listened with interest. The two processes he'd led me to before had been powerfully beneficial.

"Thanks, Werner. I haven't heard anything about the training." Do they have any introductory events? If they do, maybe I can go to one."

"As a matter of fact, they do," he replied. "I will find out the schedule and get back to you."

"Would you be willing to take the kids when I go?"

"Absolutely."

That was a different response! I got off the phone feeling nervous. Any interaction with Werner created anxiety. Could I take his gift with no intention of encouraging our relationship? I thought to myself, "Whoa, Jane, you don't even know yet whether you want to do EST."

I went to the introductory event, and it was tremendous—exciting and engaging, and feedback from the graduates was thrilling. Of course I would do the training and deal with Werner afterwards.

EST was an inspiring and profound experience indeed, led by the founder, Werner Erhard, along with his most experienced trainer, Stuart Emory. Five hundred people attended, each confronting their own resistances while exploring how the mind operates. The EST Training gave me the ability to hear and observe my thoughts rather than believe and automatically obey them as truths. It taught me powerfully that I am responsible for my life.

Today I feel embarrassed to admit that was news to me. I had believed that events and others were the major sources of my discontent. I also learned to accept what is happening rather than resist it by using a simple repeated phrase: "Choose it as it is!" The training showed me that my choices create my life, and that commitment is the key to success.

I left EST feeling like a different woman. Joyous and empowered, I was more ready than ever to expand my work and my journey as a single woman and mother. Gratefully, Werner accepted my appreciation for the gift, as well as my signals that I didn't want to continue our relationship.

My practice was both satisfying and growing. I was leading the Parents School and my women's group, doing individual and couple private sessions and offering occasional public service parenting seminars. Even so, I was still unable to comfortably afford the upkeep on my house. I tried to sell it but economic conditions were still unfavorable. After two years a woman who worked in a bank was able to secure a low interest mortgage and buy it, a huge relief for me. I found a small house in a nearby community that allowed my daughter to continue in her school.

I was also dealing with my children's overt and covert anger about leaving their home. Either avoidant or resistant, angry or unwilling, each had his or her own issues with letting go of home. Difficult as the move was, it greatly eased the financial burden that rested heavily on my shoulders. Yet, sorting through twenty years of accumulated belongings and memorabilia was time-consuming and painful. I went through photos of happier times, my sand collection, samples taken from beaches in the Caribbean and Europe, children's costumes and letters from camp, greeting cards and more. The memories were sad to relive, and it was difficult to decide whether to let go of items or keep them.

Work was a respite for me, the happiest hours of my day. It was a time to settle into myself, relax, and be of service. My clients enlarged my perspective, reminding me there was far more to life than what was happening with my family and me. They taught me daily about the complexities of life: the overcoming of repressed and undervalued parts of self, the tensions between individual and relational desires, the reclamation of sensuality in the face of shame and bias, the impact of religion on freedom, and the profound imprint of our families of origin. Clearly, our parents and siblings live powerfully in our minds and bodies, until we consciously observe and decide upon, or reject, their modeling for ourselves.

Most of all, my joy was in working with couples. I am forever amazed at how perfectly we fit with our partners, even though unconsciously. In some ways the fit is for healthy and happy reasons, and other times as repetitions of painful childhood experiences in need of resolution. In looking back on my marriage, I see that my longing to enjoy the pleasures of the world attracted me to Werner. While I fulfilled that desire, at the same time I recreated the painful inattentiveness and absence of recognition that I had endured as a child. I unconsciously gave myself another opportunity to heal those hidden wounds.

It brought me much joy to facilitate the coming together of couples as they released their individual barriers to intimacy, living in the present, first one by one, and then two by two. I also had the opportunity to guide couples through peaceful, cooperative, and considerate separation when that was their choice.

Although I celebrated the victory of creating a professional life I treasured, and I had climbed out of financial danger, I had no time, energy or access to meet people or enjoy the richness of the world. As my work life grew and financial pressures eased somewhat, I felt the restriction of my confined personal life. Although my experience was internally deep, I longed for exposure to theater, art, and concerts. I missed parties, travel, and beautiful shops. I wanted more fun. Trapped in a revolving door of private sessions and constant parenting responsibilities, and involved with a kind but limited man, I was not living the life I envisioned. I was stuck.

Ten years after leaving my marriage, I decided I could afford to return to Europe. Ron was excited to join me as I planned our trip to Portugal, a new destination for me. I had never designed a trip before, and it was empowering to do it. We visited Lisbon, Sintra, and the Algarve. I especially loved the Algarve, the beautiful sea with huge rocks rising from its depths, lovely sand, and warm sunshine.

We had a good time together—sightseeing, relaxing on the beach, experimenting with foods, interacting with Portuguese merchants, making love. Returning to Europe was my personal victory, and it was fun to witness Ron's excitement on his first trip abroad.

My initiative to travel had a dramatic impact. I learned that I could explore the world on my own terms, and that I could find resources to assist me in accomplishing my desires. A man had always laid out my itinerary, made my air and hotel reservations, and chosen the highlights to visit. This time I did all that for us. I had learned that I could navigate life at home on my own, and this trip showed me that I could manage what I needed and wanted anywhere. It was a freeing and strengthening realization. I had let go of my belief that I needed a man to take me into the world.

When I returned home in August I promised my good friend Sandy, who was in my EST seminar, that by December I would end my relationship with Ron. It was necessary to set both of us free. Ron and I were helpmates for each other. I was grateful for the friendship, support, and sexual life we shared, but I had never seen him as my life partner. It was time to go it alone, use more of my energy for myself, and perhaps open a space for a mate.

Many an evening on my solo walks I asked for guidance on how to find my way toward my vision of a balanced life of work and play, aloneness and a satisfying intimate relationship with a man who was my peer. And how can I describe my surprise when, in the midst of feeling entrapped and alone, I heard my Guides say, "No worries, Jane. The man you will marry is already known to you."

t w e n t y   t w o

BHAGWAN/OREGON

EIGHT YEARS AFTER OUR SEPARATION, WERNER BECAME A disciple of Bhagwan Shree Rajneesh, an Indian guru. He shocked me by coming to Dick's college graduation at Duke University in his disciple attire: a bright red long-sleeved tee-shirt, red jeans, and a mala bead necklace with Bhagwan's picture attached. I was appalled.

Werner's red attire was in sharp contrast to Dick, who was dressed in his preppy blue blazer, gray slacks, light blue shirt, and rep tie. I wondered how Dick felt and what his friends and classmates were thinking. I wondered how he would explain that to them and to his college professor, who had asked Dick to help write a book after graduation. Dick never said anything about the event, so I chose not to address it.

A few weeks later Werner showed up at Susan's high school graduation dressed the same way. She was extremely embarrassed, an adolescent girl so exposed to her peers. I became even more alarmed when he took our son Barry to a Bhagwan program, panicked at how his decision to become a disciple might affect our children.

Similar to my initial reaction to Werner's earlier involvement at the Casriel Institute, I decided I needed to learn about what he was doing and how it might affect our family. I chose to attend a one-week annual celebration that summer at Rancho Rajneesh in Oregon.

Bhagwan was a controversial and provocative figure who challenged basic societal norms. He taught that love is the most dangerous energy to the ego because love annihilates it; he also believed that blind acceptance of political and cultural thinking blocks us from becoming our authentic selves. Frequently attacked in the US, he was referred to as the "sex guru," teaching that sex was the kindergarten of spirituality. He taught that our societal conditioning caused us to be sexually repressed, and that until we fully experienced our natural sexuality we would be preoccupied with it, never realizing our spiritual potential.

There was considerable federal, state, and public pressure against Bhagwan. Governments were charging him with tax evasion. Neighboring communities were unhappy with the commune in their backyard. There was much suspicion and gossip about him being a charlatan and a danger to society. The commune was well funded by loyal disciples who made it possible for Bhagwan to own dozens of Rolls Royce cars. Disciples said the cars were used to confront their preoccupation with the material world, but journalists reported them as evidence that he was a con artist. I didn't know what was true. I was anxious about going to the commune yet unconcerned about how Bhagwan would affect me, quite certain I would have nothing to do with him. This all seemed so foreign to me. My concern was how this might affect my children.

I was warmly greeted when I arrived and assigned to a tent with three others. New sleeping bags were provided with shelves available for our belongings. Communal bathrooms were nearby.

Everything was immaculate. The long roads were surfaced with beautiful red gravel and were meticulously maintained.

On my first day there I developed major head congestion. Fortunately it disappeared in only two days, healing without medication. I was tired, slept much more than usual, and spent most of my time happily alone in silence. I went to morning and evening meditations with several hundred people sitting in silence, sometimes watching graceful dancers moving to exquisite lyre music. One afternoon I found a grassy shaded spot and lay down, treasuring the moist lushness and sweet smell, something I had never noticed before.

Organic fruits and vegetables were grown on site and served at well-organized and plentiful buffets. I watched disciples working cooperatively in the fields and heard them singing together. Others happily served us our nutritious meals. Guests were invited to join in whatever work tasks we desired. I worked in the kitchen and washed vegetables. It felt sweet to be with the disciples. They were relaxed, efficient, and helpful.

Although Bhagwan had been in silence for months and remained so during my entire visit, there were videos of his talks playing on large screens in many locations. They were spellbinding and funny. We were encouraged to go to a small building called the "Laughter Hut" to experience contagious laughter. When I entered I heard people laughing, which seemed strange, but after a few minutes I found myself laughing, too. I felt embarrassed and silly, but it was good to be laughing for no reason. Disciples and guests lined the road waiting for Bhagwan each afternoon when he took a slow drive around the grounds in a Rolls Royce. He looked deeply into each person's eyes, but I didn't feel anything unusual in those moments.

Life was different at the commune: peaceful, safe, loving, orderly and slow—strikingly slow. The energy was unknown to me, like magic air. I cannot explain how it felt to be in Bhagwan's presence. He lived and modeled life as meditation. I think his purpose was to free us from the limited belief that we were only physical bodies and acculturated minds. His silent presence directly connected me to my soul. I could feel myself shifting. The power of peace and kindness was deep and intense, and the freedom I felt was indescribably joyous. I had fallen into a state of love.

Towards the end of the week, I had an unforgettable moment of lightness as I skipped down the road, free as a young girl. I came across a stand of sunflowers and stopped to cup one in my hands. For many minutes I burrowed my head into the flower, allowing its large yellow petals to surround my face with its seeds pressing against my nose and cheeks. I felt we were merged, as one. Afterwards I realized that I had been totally unselfconscious, absorbed only in the feeling. How did that happen? As I walked back to my tent I remembered the awe I felt seeing the vast sunflower fields in Italy, stretching as far as my eyes could see, each looking up to the sun.

I was uneasy when it was time to go home. Feeling like a changed person, I wondered how I would relate to my family. How would I relate to the world? Would this feeling last? If it did, how long could it last? At the airport I found myself in a quandary. Scores of Bhagwan's disciples were there dressed in orange garb. I was wearing my normal street clothes, appearing conventional. I noticed many travelers looking askance at the disciples, whispering in seemingly superior judgment. There I was, one of the orange people in my heart, looking like the "normal ones," yet knowing keenly which group was mine.

For a while I condemned myself for my pretense, but I eventually came to accept that, although I was able to experience a new and sacred inner reality, I did not want a commune lifestyle for myself or my children. I did not want us to live in a different society. I wanted to open myself spiritually, emotionally, and sexually. I aspired to bring a more loving me to my world, yet I was concerned about how I would function. The world was vastly different, filled with ambition, competitiveness, and aggression. Despite being drawn to Bhagwan's spiritual energy and teachings, I remained concerned about the controversy that swirled around him. I did not want to engage with those distractions. I trusted my reluctance, took what served me, left the rest, and never returned to the commune.

I stayed in an elevated state for almost three months, slowly watching my expansiveness close down, unable to prevent it. I did not have the tools to keep myself that open. Such a state was unsustainable on my own, yet the memory kept urging me inward.

I was still concerned that Werner might decide to move there and encourage the children to join him, but his time as a disciple was short-lived. He left Bhagwan within months and became interested in another growth process. The children seemed to accept his choices without question, expressing little interest in any of them. I was relieved that they would safely maintain their lives at home in our culture. Committed to continue my spiritual development in my way, I would do my best to be a mindful and loving mother.

As the years went by, startling dramas discrediting Bhagwan became public. I still don't know whether the ugly stories in the news were true. He was eventually imprisoned, then deported from the US, and he died in India in 1991. I felt great sadness, but also much gratitude for the week I spent with him and the years of spiritual growth he initiated. Sometimes I read Bhagwan's books and listen to his audios about ancient religions and spiritual masters. They still nourish me, as does the music that uplifts me as I remember.

Having that extended experience of bliss transformed my life. I discovered a place inside that I didn't know was there. I learned that I am capable of profound happiness, just me, with myself. I could experience happiness on my own and in relationship. I learned that my happiness sourced in my connection to the Divine, and that the more I live from my soul, the happier I am. It is still my purpose to stay in contact with my soul and find ways to express it in the world.

Werner brought Casriel, bio-energetics, EST, and Bhagwan to my life. I am supremely thankful, for they were all powerful steps on my inner journey. His Bhagwan choice was bold, unusual, and scary, and like a lioness with her cubs, I felt a strong instinct to protect my children. That turned out to be unnecessary, but in the end, my desire to protect them actually served me.

twenty three

BOB BEGINNINGS

I MET BOB WHEN I WAS 23 AND LIKED HIM FROM THE START. He was easy to be with, handsome, generous, and smart. I admired his tastes, shared his sensibilities, and respected his worldly strengths. I always felt Bob's pleasure in my company and I in his.

We lived in the same building in White Plains, New York. Actually we had the same apartment, mine on the second floor and his on the fifth. I had introduced myself to his wife Elin in the park as she tended their daughter Shelley, a toddler about the same age as my son Bill.

Bob seemed settled and happy, successful and confident in his work. He was home every night for dinner and encouraged hiring babysitters so that he and Elin could have date nights. That was in sharp contrast to my marriage where my husband worked late, traveled extensively, used weekends to recover from his exhaustion, and did not prioritize our time together.

Elin and Bob bought a house and moved from the apartment building before we did. They became involved in their new community and our children went to different schools. When we moved to our house we stayed in touch but saw them far less. We weren't as close, and they weren't aware of the extent of my marital difficulties.

After I separated from Werner I visited Elin during the day when I could. At that time it was unusual for couples to socialize with singles and neither Bob nor I reached out to stay in contact. As my work life grew I had less time to visit and gradually lost touch with Elin too. Years later I received a call from Shelley that her Mom was close to death and that she thought I would want to attend her funeral.

I went to the funeral with Werner and was amazed to see more than a hundred people there. I wondered who they were, knowing that Elin did not have a wide circle of friends. It turned out that this was a joint funeral since Elin's father had died in a different New York hospital on the same day. Family and friends of both, and many of Bob's business associates, attended. Sitting there with Werner I noticed Bob as I remembered him: composed, quiet, and refined. We said hello, but he was occupied and distant. I thought about the many evenings we shared as couples, the laughs, the movies, dinners, the games and conversations. I thought about agreeing to be guardian for their children who were now adults. It was strange to see Shelley, Ken, and Amy whom I hadn't seen since they were adolescents. I wondered how Bob was, and how the children were handling Elin's death. I decided I would contact him to visit while they were still in town.

Weeks later when I called Bob, he seemed delighted to hear from me. The deep affection that we had for each other as young married friends was immediately present. He invited me to his home for dinner that Friday night with his daughter, his future son-in-law, and sister.

It felt so perfectly natural to be there, like family. How many times had I been in this home—sat at their table as a guest, felt free to go into their refrigerator, played Scrabble or bridge, attended children's birthday parties, and watched the first Super Bowl. Now that Bob and I were both single, we were free to feel the strong attraction between us that was immediate and obvious.

After dinner Bob's family left and we talked into the early morning hours. We shared intimately about the challenging events each had lived through in recent years. He told me about his work and how it sustained him during his journey with Elin's long illness. He talked about his fear when she had a stroke in her final days and could speak only gibberish. He said he had been so involved with Elin's doctors and hospitals for so many months that he was uncertain how he would navigate his personal life.

I told him about my family counseling and parent education work, my deep interest in the inner life, my divorce, and the painful financial situation that followed. Bob expressed his regret that he hadn't been there to help when I was struggling. I explained my ten-year relationship with Ron with whom I had a gratifying friendship and sexual life, as I raised my children and created my career. I told Bob that it was always clear to me that Ron would never be my life partner. During those years my primary focus was to grow up, raise my children, and become an autonomous, independent woman.

Bob and I sat at right angles in his beautiful family room; a square end table nestled in the corner between us, each with our hands resting on the arms of our chairs. After a couple of hours, slowly, slowly, our fingertips met. Neither mentioned that moment but it was an electrically charged event. We continued our conversation in that connection, neither of us moving. When I was leaving, Bob asked if I would like to come back for dinner the next Friday. As he gave me a goodnight hug I asked, "Are you up for risking our friendship as it is?" He replied, "Absolutely."

Our times together were exciting and stimulating as Bob was surprisingly direct and revealing. I was happy to engage in his level of openness, yet terrified of trusting a man with whom I could possibly have a lifetime partnership. I was embarrassed at dinner one evening when, as I was going on about Robert Kennedy's assassination, he asked me if I really wanted to talk about politics. I had to admit that it felt safer. I was attracted to Bob and was moved by his choice to comfortably express his vulnerabilities, one of which was sexual inactivity. Bob and Elin's marriage had major problems long before Elin's terminal illness. In fact, her metastatic cancer had caused them to spend far more time together than they had before, as they dealt with doctors and hospitals.

It was November and I had promised myself and told my friend Sandy that I would end my relationship with Ron by year-end. I decided that this was the time to take that step. Even though it was honest and necessary, I still felt sad. Ron had been a devoted companion through my most difficult time.

Driving on Pleasantville Road toward home after another of our lovely dinners together, Bob said, "Would you like to come back to my house for a drink?"

My body went into alarm mode as fear overtook me. I didn't know what to say. I wanted to spend more time with him but wasn't ready for sex. After a long pause I said, "Please pull over and stop so I can think about it."

I could tell Bob was surprised, but he quickly obliged. After several minutes of silence, during which he waited patiently, he asked, "What's going on?"

"I want to be with you but I'm not ready for sex and don't want to put either of us in an awkward position."

Bob took my hand and said, "That's fine, honey. Let's just go back to the house and have a drink."

The evening ended as I hoped, warmly and happily. I learned early on to just tell Bob my truth moment by moment.

We saw each other often, and our times together were always

fun and relaxed. With a growing connection, sex was a natural outcome. Bob was delighted to have a pleasurable sex life again, feeling at ease as I communicated my desires. I was delighted to be with a man who met me so completely. Our times together were mutually satisfying and wonderful.

A few weeks later Bob called, excited about an idea. "Let's go down to Florida, visit our mothers separately, and then fly to Paradise Island together." Since both of us were uneasy visiting our mothers, this seemed like a great idea. I was not willing to accept the trip as a gift, insisting that I pay what I could afford towards the expenses. Bob saw that as unnecessary but heard my need for independence. He accepted my plan.

Although this trip was a hugely tempting offer, it also scared me. I was afraid of living together, even for four days, concerned about how I would feel with no private time or space, afraid of that level of intimacy.

Paradise Island was the most idyllic trip of my life. We stayed at a small, luxurious hotel situated on a magnificent crushed coral beach that was always cool to the touch. Clear, calm, aqua water was beautiful to look at and easy to be in. I can still remember the feeling of Bob standing in the water holding me close, with my legs wrapped around his body. We went to town and to Nassau, had beautiful meals, and made love often. One afternoon we took a nap and asked the desk for a 3:00 pm wake-up call to visit the straw market. The call never came. The operator had confused our request, and the phone rang at 3:00 am instead, waking us from a deep sleep. When I realized what had happened, I just laughed. Bob found that totally charming.

We walked the beach holding hands, sat on the deck drinking luscious pineapple smoothies, and had many interesting conversations. I told Bob that I saw my path as owning my strengths, and his as opening his heart and loving. That vision turned out to be the blueprint of our future lives.

We left Paradise Island in a paradise of our own, and Bob asked how I felt about living together. His house was on the market. He had planned to move to an apartment in New York City, but now he wanted to stay close by. I invited him to live with me. Bob was delighted!

A little while later he said, "I am so happy that we will be living together! How can I contribute? Of course, I want to pay at least my share of the household expenses."

Holding tightly onto my separateness and independence and still unable to trust I said, "No, Bob. Thanks but these are my expenses and I can handle them."

Not at all comfortable with my reply, Bob said, laughing, "I have never been a kept man before. Let's talk about this another time. In the meantime, I am thrilled to live with you, and I will pay for a cleaning woman to come in weekly." I happily accepted that with big hugs and kisses. Looking back on my vulnerable, self-protective requests, I am still touched by how graciously he accepted the steps that I needed to take to become his partner.

One evening we went to a local Chinese restaurant where Bob asked me to marry him. It was no surprise, other than the location. After the beauty of Paradise Island and the many lavish city and country restaurants we frequented, this nondescript eatery became the most special place on the planet. It was easy for me to say "YES" wholeheartedly. I had come a long way in letting go of my fears, and Bob had given me more loving attention than I ever thought possible. We were both in love and divinely happy.

Bob agreed to do his own laundry, and we laughed as he routinely hit his head on the top of the stairwell on his way to the basement. My house was too small for him. It was out of scale for his size, both physically and energetically. He suggested that we buy a house together with the proceeds from my home, with him supplying the balance needed. He also said he did not believe in prenuptial agreements and offered a plan where, over many years, we would equalize our assets. Given our financial differential, it took much stretching to expand into and even think of receiving that degree of wealth for myself. While it might seem like an easy thank you, it was extremely difficult for me to accept his extraordinary generosity. It still moves me to this day.

Because our tastes and sensibilities are very much aligned, looking for a home was easy. For quite a while neither of us was excited with anything we saw. One night I had a dream that pictured the interior of a spacious house with large rooms, high cathedral ceilings, a winding staircase in the bedroom, two work spaces, and a balcony overlooking the living room. It was beautiful. Within a week, our realtor brought us to a home that exactly matched my dream. It was located in a development that did not please us, but the interior was so perfect for our needs that we decided to buy it. We hosted our wedding there before moving in.

I enjoyed our wedding planning even though I felt the pressure of doing my counseling practice and carrying all these details in my head. It was challenging to meet with suppliers during their workdays and ours. One afternoon Bob had scheduled several of them to come for consultations in short intervals. Rushing from decisions on menus to flowers, music to photography, we had consecutive meetings, none of which felt complete or enjoyable. This was not my pace, nor my pleasure. It was the first time I had come up against Bob's "businessman" persona, making decisions driven by time and money rather than pleasure. It was a side of him I had never seen.

As we sat in the car I started to cry and said, "I am so disappointed. I was looking forward to making our wedding plans. These meetings felt more like business, about just getting the job done. Not fun."

I don't think Bob really understood my upset. I went on to say, "I want to enjoy every step of designing our wedding. I want everything we do together to be a pleasure!"

Bob was quiet and after a short while, he apologized. I could tell that he felt sad. He never wanted to disappoint me.

I shopped for a wedding dress for some time and finally found one that I liked. It was ivory satin with diamond-like beads and two graceful rows of flounces, far more costly than I was comfortable with. I told Bob about it, and he insisted that I buy it. With tears streaming down my cheeks, I accepted. Stretching into abundance was so difficult.

On the day of the wedding we went to a hotel close to our home where we would dress and spend the night. I felt anxious, and as the day wore on I became increasingly agitated. My agitation escalated into a panic unlike any I had experienced before or since. Nothing Bob said or I told myself calmed me. I went for a long walk and expended some nervous energy, attempting to find the source of what was so scary. I was afraid of imprisoning myself again. My experience of marriage had been so painful, both to be in and to leave. I was still afraid to trust a man.

As soon as my daughter Susan arrived at the house I settled down. She was excited: "I am so happy for you, Mom. Happy that you are marrying Bob."

I took that as reassurance that despite my fears, I was taking a good step for myself. I knew she would have told me long before if she was concerned.

I told her, "I know this is crazy, but I am scared to get married again."

"I get it, but let me help you get dressed, and you'll feel better."

I breathed in her calming presence, and we laughed together as she helped me dress and ready myself for my wedding ceremony and party. She is always a balm to my spirit.

It was a beautiful September evening. All seven of our children were attendants, and our parents, families, and friends were present to celebrate us. We spoke the vows we had created, and the band played our favorite music. We ended the service exiting to "Life Is a Celebration with You on My Arm," a song from *La Cage Aux Folles*, the first Broadway show we had seen together. I danced all evening, especially enjoying my time with Bob's son Ken, who until that point had kept his distance. We danced to "Jump," flinging our arms in the air each time we heard jump. Although he has since passed on, I will always remember the joy we shared that day. Bob was attentive to how things were going with the caterers but since this was our day to rejoice, I encouraged him to let that go and play with me. He did, and we were both supremely happy!

We went to Italy and France for our honeymoon. It was important to me to return to the Italian villa where I had spent the summer sixteen years earlier. I knew that going there with Bob would be healing. It was a pleasure to take him to the house, the town, the shops, and the neighboring resorts that I frequented at a far less happy time. We bought some pottery souvenirs to mark the visit. I left feeling grateful that I'd had lovely times there with my young children and now again with my new husband.

Then we were off to France where the highlight for me was a drive from the Riviera through the wine country. We enjoyed clear, warm days filled with sunshine and flowers, lovemaking, and revealing conversation. I drew Bob a verbal picture of the dream marriage I wanted us to create. We would share our desires, feelings, visions, passions, and love. We spoke about what all those possibilities meant while driving through the gorgeous French countryside. We ate scrumptious food at world-renowned restaurants. We stayed in elegant and interesting old hotels. My favorite was a small castle, where we walked up a steep circular staircase to our spacious room in the turret.

Bob came into my life at the perfect time. Through ten years of intensive inner work I had transformed my dependence to independence, a goal I had set before ever considering a lifetime partnership. I did not need a partner, but I now desired one. I had put my heart and soul into my growth and felt rewarded for taking the risk of leaving a marriage that lacked love, respect, and attention, even though it gave me security. My greatest victory was finding the love and security I yearned for inside myself.

Our time as newlyweds was as magical as the day we came together. I never imagined that I would feel such enchantment, peace, and love. I was now seen, known, and treasured. Bob reflected my beauty and femininity and widened my worldly experience. I deepened his inner world in ways he gratefully accepted, bringing him to new emotions and sensations. We were both ecstatic and growing.

twenty four

PROUD MOTHER

LOOKING BACK I SEE THAT DESPITE MY TROUBLED FIRST MAR-
riage, I found beautiful blessings in motherhood throughout
that time. My goal was that each of my children felt cared for,
known, and loved.

When they were young it was easy. I loved being around
them and found them adorable. Their energy, purity, creativity,
laughter, and curiosity uplifted me. They interested me, and I
learned from them. It was a delight to move through the stages
of infancy, toddler, and first school experiences. It was more difficult to watch them grow into their own individuality through
middle school, junior high, and high school as their lives became
more complex. Their challenges increased: social groups, sports
teams, sibling rivalries. Other family members, friends and teachers made their own impressions on them over which I had no
control. It was difficult when I saw them hurt. It pleased me to
support their independence, allowing them to make more of
their own decisions and become more self-sufficient. In time
they would need to make all of their decisions.

For me, the biggest challenge of raising children was to know when and where to let them lead. After infancy, children push more for their ideas in each stage of development. How much protection and guidance is needed? How much freedom? When is it in their best interest to be involved and when is it best to let them make decisions and deal with the consequences? When is their genuine self-speaking? When does the influence of their peer group press on them? When are they being obedient just to stay in my good graces? Parenting requires deep listening, not only to words, but also to subtle emotional shifts.

I wanted my children to feel happy. It required wisdom and humility to realize that they may have better and more authentic answers than I had for them. With each step they took on their own, it became obvious that they were separate beings and that I was simply their guardian along the way. This was increasingly true from their first physical step to the day they left home. They decided their direction. I found that both a joy and a sorrow. I was happy for their strength and independence and to have more time for myself to grow as an individual, yet they were moving away, leaving a bigger space between us stage by stage.

As I became more soul selfish, sometimes I made choices that differed from what my children were accustomed to or wanted, and they did not easily accept that. I felt the tension my shift had created. I am still not certain how that change lives in each of them today. Did they see me as soul selfish or just plain selfish? I notice differences in how each one decides about the degree they are willing to prioritize their soul choices. Did my shift in inner direction encourage them to stand more for their souls, or is their childhood pain still hindering their freedom?

One of the things I learned about parenting is that there is no such thing as divorce. Although I was far more present in my children's daily experience than their Dad was, I frequently see his influence in my adult children. He continues to live in their minds and hearts, even in their mannerisms. Clearly, each parent—in marriage or divorce, present or absent—leaves a legacy.

Looking back on my family life, I see a rhythm of expansion and contraction from young newlyweds, growing to a family of three, four, five, and six. After divorce, five of us lived together and when my oldest son went off to college, four, then three, two, and one. Then I was alone. And then, once again, my family began to grow when I remarried.

Bob had three children. Being a step-parent was very different than being a parent. His children related to me adult to adult, more as their Dad's wife even though I had known them since childhood. They saw me as a friend of their family and had some pleasant memories. They did not look to me as their mother even though their Mom was deceased. Bob's daughter Shelley was the first to become a parent, giving us our first grandson. Six of our seven children now have children of their own. The ebb and flow of all these changes taught me more than ever that no matter who is in my present experience, this is my life.

Watching my children parent their children, I feel grateful that they have chosen to continue many of my practices and, of course, added many of their own. Naturally their mates' backgrounds and ideas are major factors in my grandchildren's lives. Freedom has been my yardstick, silently accepting their decisions whether I agree or not. I remind myself that I had my turn and now it is theirs; another opportunity for letting go.

Relating to my adult children still challenges my "good girl," knowing when and how to express my feelings about their choices that involve me. It is still uncomfortable for me to stand for myself and tell them my desires, or explain when and why I disagree or am disappointed.

I am proud to say that all four of my children are in good health, are devoted to their marriages and families, have created prospering careers, and maintain long-standing friendships. I am grateful that they and their mates have brought me six wonderful grandchildren. They have widened and deepened my life by inviting me into their interests and successes, including me in their worlds of sports, public policy, film, and technology.

One of my favorite recollections of motherhood was the fiftieth birthday party that my children gave me. Bill and Susan, who lived nearby, did much to make it a beautiful event, and Dick and Barry came from out of town to celebrate. I had just come together with Bob, who was there with his daughter, Shelley. His presence felt like a reward for all the risks I had taken. Having my four children honor me with this party filled my heart. They invited close friends and family, even my former husband and his fiancée. It was a party filled with love and happiness.

When my gorgeous whipped cream–covered birthday cake was presented, I stood and held it as my guests sang to me. After blowing out the candles and thrilled with the applause, I looked down and saw that whipped cream covered the top of my bright red dress. I just laughed, feeling so high that nothing could embarrass me or diminish my joy.

There I was in the home I had bought and renovated on my own, being honored with this beautiful birthday party by my four children, all in their twenties. My new man was present, and we were looking forward to building a life together. Friends and family were there to share my happiness. I don't think anyone in that room could possibly imagine the victory this milestone was for me.

twenty five

CASA DE CAMPO

MARRIED LIFE WAS DIVINE. THE BLOOM OF NEW LOVE PER-
meated our lives and our home, and we were each happy in our
work. Our evenings and weekends were filled with friends, family,
parties, theater, dinners, and most of all, each other.

My only concern was personal space. My days were occupied
with work that ended at 7:00 pm. Bob usually bounded into the
house at 7:15 ready for our evening together. After a while I began
to feel crowded, needing time to switch gears and check in with
myself. I wanted some room to digest the day and freshen up,
but felt pressure while he waited for me.

When I expressed my discomfort, Bob surprised me by asking
if I was willing to cut back on my work. He said that reducing my
income would not impact our lifestyle and I would have more
time for myself during the day while he was working.

His idea posed a dilemma. While I desired more time for
myself, I also loved my work. It satisfied me spiritually, emotionally, and intellectually, and it protected me from ever again
being financially dependent on any man. Bob gently reminded

me that we have a world of choices open to us and that I would still have my work, just a bit less of it. He thought that would be better for me and for us. Although I knew his idea made sense, I felt extremely uneasy.

The same fear of joining my life with a man that overtook me on my wedding day resurfaced. Since then I have succeeded in becoming more trusting, but at that time Bob was suggesting I do what was most scary, to let go of my need for financial independence. It had taken me ten years to build financial security following my devastating divorce settlement, and I believed it was crucial for me to maintain it. Although money was no longer a problem in my life, it was the place I felt most vulnerable. Despite gratefully and happily receiving Bob's generosity, financially I was still thinking like a single woman, earning and investing my money separately, holding onto my safety.

Bob was asking me to marry him on another level. He wanted to contribute more financially so that I could have more pleasure separately and we could have more time and fun together. It was as if he had drawn a beautiful bubble bath in which I could luxuriate, but when I put my toe in the water it felt uncomfortably hot. Perhaps I could test the waters and gradually get used to his idea. Could I let go of my fear and super-responsibility and try to grasp more pleasure?

Pleasure...I already had much pleasure in my life. My commitment to growth and responsibility brought me great pleasure, and this beautiful marriage too! At last I felt that I was an authentic, responsible, soul-connected woman. Although I was having fun, I had not prioritized it. Bob was asking me to let go of some of my work to give myself and us more play time. I thought, "Perhaps play and pleasure are my next soul selfish step. I could begin to explore that." After much discomfort and deliberation, I decided I would take the risk and slowly started cutting back on my sessions.

A year after our wedding Bob received an invitation from a business associate offering us a one-week stay in January at their company's villa in the Dominican Republic. It was in the beautiful Casa de Campo resort and would be a welcome winter break from the cold Northeast. Of course I gave the invitation a big "YES," cleared my client calendar long in advance, and took off to another Caribbean paradise. The villa was spacious and gorgeous, within walking distance of a beach backed by exquisite palm trees overlooking an inviting turquoise sea. Attendants were on duty to offer towels, cool drinks, and any assistance we desired. There were tennis courts and a well-laid-out golf course, far beyond my capabilities. Eating outdoors with balmy breezes caressing my skin was a sensual gift. Sometimes I felt like pinching myself to make certain this was all real.

Four days into the trip Bob's assistant contacted him with news that we were invited to ride in a private railroad car from Chicago to San Diego to attend the Super Bowl and pre-game festivities. The owner of a company Bob did business with had recently purchased a Pullman and dining car, and he had hired a talented chef for the trip. We would need to leave for Chicago to board the train immediately after returning to New York. Neither of us had ever been on a long train ride, much less attended a Super Bowl. Bob was eager to accept. I was familiar with football too, having gone to New York Giants' games for many years. Even though it sounded exciting, I felt tension growing in my stomach again.

How can I do this? Here I am in the Caribbean taking a week off from work, with my clients expecting to resume their sessions next week. How can I call them to say that I am going on yet another vacation? How responsible or professional is that?

At first I said, "No," thinking it outrageous to take another week off. Bob urged me to give myself the fun of this trip. He talked to me for hours, attempting to convince me that this was a great opportunity for something we might never have a chance to do again. When I told him that none of my clients were in crisis, he replied they would understand and accept a one-week delay in resuming their sessions. I wanted to believe him, but the idea was difficult for me to accept.

I then called my daughter Susan who has always been my teacher in play, while also being reliable and grounded. She saw the choice as a no-brainer. She said, "Mom, your clients will be fine for one more week. What would happen if you got sick and couldn't see them? Would they accept that? Of course they would. So why wouldn't they accept your good fortune as readily as they would your sickness?" I took another look at my thinking, then yielded to Bob and Susan, trusting their love for me more than my own.

Susan agreed to call each client on my calendar and in every instance got positive responses. They were uniformly excited for me, delighted for my opportunity. Several were also generous in telling her how much they valued their work with me and to please wish me a wonderful time. I felt relieved, touched, and honored.

The train ride was fantastic. Twelve of us bonded on the 2½ day trip, hanging out and getting to know each other. We had interesting conversations about our professional lives, favorite movies, and vacation spots in the world and US, and funny stories about our families and children. We climbed around tiny compartments to our bunk beds and pocket-sized bathroom. At dinner we laughed as we watched the soup swish back and forth in our bowls, wondering whether it would overflow. Leaving the wintry Midwest behind, we traveled through the plains and snow-capped Rocky Mountains into the warmth and beauty of the southwest. I was standing outdoors on the back of the train with the warm breeze gently blowing through my hair and the sun on my shoulders when we approached the Pacific Ocean.

Our long journey was almost over. When we arrived in San Diego, it was a luxury to check into a hotel with a king-sized bed and full bathroom!

Actually, the train ride was far more fun than the pre–Super Bowl festivities or the one-sided game. We were invited to several "hoopla" parties where I found the huge displays of food and alcohol garish and the crowds and noise overwhelming. I did enjoy seeing Chuck Berry perform, and Bob got to have a conversation with Gayle Sayers, one of his football heroes.

I had an extraordinary time during that week, happy that I got out of my own way and gave myself permission to go. After we flew home I decided to make my pleasure a higher priority. I opened my calendar and, with a bold magic marker, boxed out personal time before I made any new work appointments. I committed myself to more play and pleasure, happily leaving space to accept new opportunities on my soul selfish journey.

twenty six

PARENTS ON THE JOB

IN THE 1990S, WHEN MOTHERS WERE PROUDLY RUSHING back to work, I developed a corporate seminar program that I named "Parents on the Job." Using the same meditation process I had used a decade earlier for the Parents School, I created three- and six-session programs dealing with parenting skills and balancing work and family responsibilities. This gave me the opportunity to enlarge my professional life while supporting working parents.

Mothers were torn by conflicting demands, feeling guilty that they were not giving enough to their children, jobs, or marriages. It was simply too much. The mothers who had the most angst were not those who had to work for economic reasons, but rather those who chose to work for their own fulfillment.

Creating the program was easy and fun. I asked a former Parents School participant to work with me. We enjoyed downloading tapes from the school and lifting nuggets from my meditation transcripts for the new seminars. Marketing, a new skill set for me, was far more challenging. At that time "Parents on the Job" was a brand new idea, a conceptual and financial risk for companies. Again listening within, I was guided to put my focus on contribution rather than selling. This made marketing much easier for me, since I trusted that the programs would definitely benefit both working parents and companies.

As a family counselor always dealing with intangibles, I found it exciting to work with visual projects: designing a logo, brochures, stationery, and business cards to send out to the world. Friends furnished contacts in several large companies, and after repeated calls and months of following up, I began to hear interest. My first seminar was scheduled at Pitney Bowes, recommended by a Board member of Wainwright House, a prestigious human resource center in Rye, New York, where I was chairperson at the time. Several other major national and international corporations followed.

This work gave me a glimpse into the corporate world and an opportunity to support up to 50 participants at a time in strengthening their abilities in work and parenting. I emphasized self-care and the necessity of creating back-up support; I also taught the importance of listening to children's thoughts, feelings, interests, and talents. Regardless of the company, I heard the same story over and over: burned out women on their own, or with little help from mates who assumed the role of "assistant parent" at best. The discussions remained primarily on a pragmatic level: "How do I get myself and my children out on time in the morning? How do I deal with reentry after a stressful day at the office? How do I find free time when my children want my attention? How can I deal better with my children's misbehavior? What do I do when my boss wants me to stay late?" All were valid and worthy questions.

The forums offered useful parenting strategies despite obstacles. Participants were obviously reluctant to be open with workmates, especially since the groups included some women in management. This significantly limited the depth of discussion. Seminars were an hour long and conflicting meetings often prevented participants from attending regularly. Sometimes executives used class times as public relations opportunities to promote their company's liberal family policy.

Two years after beginning "Parents on the Job" I received a call from a Fortune 500 company asking for a meeting. I expected them to inquire about the program, but instead they were interested in the possibility of doing "Parents on the Job" on a national level. Their idea was for me to train their trainers to present the seminars. I was flattered by the acknowledgement and listened intently, understanding that this would be entirely different work. We ended the meeting with each open to considering the idea, but I left feeling unsettled.

Although I believed that it would be a great service to train trainers and would offer me significant financial rewards, I was not excited. Repeating the same material over and over was not my calling. Even if I created new programs, I would still be doing repetitive trainings. I did not want that. This realization led me to think about why I had created "Parents on the Job" seminars since I had been finding those seminars were also becoming repetitive. Was it simply to enlarge my professional life? Was it to serve more parents?

I realized that I wanted some work time out of my office, to impact larger groups of people, and to learn how to promote myself on my own. Not holding my father's, brother's, Werner's, or Bob's hand, I wanted to propel myself into the world with my own energy, talents, and abilities. Creating corporate seminars on a subject in which I felt highly qualified seemed like a worthwhile endeavor.

My mind flashed back to my childhood, walking the streets of New York City feeling somewhat overwhelmed, wondering what happened inside those tall buildings. Who was in them?

What were people doing there? What was I missing? I thought about visiting Werner in his office, noticing the interactions and teamwork. I wanted to know what that felt like.

Calling myself back to the present and more fully understanding my motivations, my question became: Why was I feeling so conflicted and nervous? The possibility of doing national trainings would likely be a huge professional and financial success. I would get to travel to new places and meet many people, a big difference from my private practice. It was tempting to think about, yet I felt an uncomfortable gnawing sensation in my stomach. What would most deeply satisfy me?

The discomfort I felt thinking about training trainers also led me to see that my enthusiasm for "Parents on the Job" had waned. The corporate format was simply not conducive to the inner process that I treasure. It was my deep inner work with individuals and groups that most interested me and made me happy.

I never did work with trainers. I completed my contracts for "Parents on the Job" and turned my full attention back to my counseling practice. For twenty-nine beautiful years I spent many hours every workday focused inward. Listening to my clients and listening within, I allowed my knowledge, intuition, and guidance to flow, never knowing what would come through me. What I did know was that it benefitted my clients and nourished my soul. Nothing felt as peaceful and natural in my life.

twenty seven

BOB'S TRAUMA

AFTER OUR WEDDING, BOB AND I HAD TWO IDYLLIC YEARS OF love and intimacy, beyond anything I had ever known. He brought pleasure, comfort, and support to me and I brought love, appreciation and sexual freedom to him. We were extremely happy together.

This was during the late 1980s when personal computers became an essential part of business, and for some, everyday life. In our third year together, Bob's catalog business, the largest of its type, was gravely impacted as its biggest customers bought computers and began to do their own design and production work. Believing they would no longer need his agency's services, they offered jobs to several of Bob's talented staff. Loyal as his employees were, they also saw the reality of the fast-changing industry; coordinators, art directors, writers, and technical experts left the company, choosing to accept jobs with customers. Bob was alarmed at the speed and scope of this change, so much so that he became concerned about the viability of the company he had managed for more than fifteen years.

As Bob's business problems mounted, his frame of mind plummeted. For the first time it became clear to me, as he began to doubt his worth, that his identity was inseparably tied to his business success. Suffering from anxiety and depression, he realized that he had two choices. Either he took on the enormous challenge of technologically transforming the company and creating a different business model, or he needed to bring in a new management team and gradually retire. Both were major life changes that filled him with conflict.

It felt like I was married to a different man. Bob became more isolated. My love was barely received, and his was hidden beneath his depression. Gone was his interest in what was happening with me, my work, or my desires. Gone was his involvement in our life, our plans, play, or sex. The computer became his evening activity. After we went out socially he came home, went upstairs, and worked on his computer. When we had dinner at home, he went upstairs afterward and worked on his computer. Once in a while I noticed that he was playing solitaire and wondered how often he did that.

Eventually he went into therapy and took antidepressant medications that helped little, other than to level his mood to a constant dullness. There was no way to get through to the source of his problem as he refused to talk about what he was thinking and feeling. Instead he continued to give more of his time and attention to his business and his computer. I felt heavy-hearted, living with a man whose self-protective behaviors were making him disappear before my eyes. It was a tragedy, since I knew that Bob was so much more than a CEO running a successful company.

I went to bed alone, often slept alone. I attempted to introduce sensual newness, even reading books that I thought would lift us both, but he was in no frame of mind to engage. Over a period of months, followed by years, I became increasingly saddened and frustrated.

Although Bob was incapable of expressing love and happiness, I never doubted his love for me. He admired and respected me, even adored me. He was happiest when he was with me but it was his fear—not his love—that dominated. He perceived his dreaded failure as bigger than himself. As his business continued to suffer, so did his strength and his sense of manhood. How long would this go on? How long could I hang in with him? How sad for Bob. How depriving for me.

Finally Bob made the choice to retire. He realized that his business concerns were jeopardizing our marriage and that turning the company around was more than he was willing to undertake. He decided to hire two men to work with him: an advanced management and technology expert and a proven salesman. The three of them worked well together. As he became comfortable with their abilities and teamwork, he promoted the management expert to replace him as CEO and took on the title of chairman. He then created a brilliant four-year exit strategy that led to his retirement.

Even with all that preparation, it was still a difficult adjustment for Bob. Who was he without his position and success? It was the way he had always given himself value. What would he do that would provide self-respect and status in the world? Who would he be if he were not producing something and earning large sums of money? What would he do that would provide the same interest and passion?

Bob looked to me to make it better. Rooted in my nurturing, feminine role and grounded in my counseling work, I took it on. Feeling very sad that he was depressed, I wanted to support him. I was also motivated to regain what I had lost. Just as I parented Mom so that she might love and parent me, I was attempting to help Bob process his issues so that he would again be free to be my partner. Yet it seemed that the more I tended to Bob's problems, the more problems there were to attend to.

I was depleted, not taking sufficient care of myself, not giving myself what I needed. Our life was about Bob's problems and our troubled marriage. There was little pleasure, yet I kept trying to help him.

As his new work team began to address the company's significant problems, Bob was able to take some time off. He had been to Egypt many years earlier and wanted to share that experience with me. He went to great lengths to plan a fascinating trip.

I will never forget driving in a cab from the Cairo airport to our hotel in Giza. Looking to the left through the dense smog I saw faint outlines of huge triangular forms beyond the shacks alongside the road. In disbelief I asked, "Are those the pyramids?" Indeed they were! The pyramids were the view from our hotel room window, and the next morning we went to explore them. It is still a mystery as to how they were built; how was each massive stone lifted? From there we went to the Sphinx. I took in the immense sculpture in awe. As I stood transfixed, I saw a cobalt blue aura several feet high surrounding it.

We took camel rides and day trips to Cairo to tour the breathtaking museum. We navigated crowded streets, fighting the unruly traffic. I was even grazed by a passing car. Flying south along the Nile we saw wide stripes of green where the river flooded, bordered by straight lines of desert sand as far as the eye could see. We visited the ancient temples, palaces, and obelisks of Luxor. When we visited the Valley of the Queens an old man sitting in front of a cave offered to usher us in for a few Egyptian pounds. He reflected the sunlight with a mirror onto the inside cave walls toward the exquisite paintings for us to see. Because the climate is so dry, they were as vibrant as when they were painted 3,500 years ago. We sailed in a felucca in Aswan and saw the bluest sky in the world. Then we flew down to Abu Simbel. Coming around a bend we saw the most magnificent and awesome statues imaginable. They were so immense and beautiful that we easily understood why the ancient people worshipped them as gods. This was the most fascinating trip of my life. I felt replenished, grateful, and happy, fully enjoying myself with Bob.

When we returned home Bob saw that the management team was progressing. It was obvious that his presence was not needed and perhaps not even welcomed. Faced with that difficult realization, he was again challenged to move on.

twenty eight

ARIZONA

BOB WANTED US TO HAVE A SECOND HOME, A PLACE THAT
we could go during the cold, drab, penetrating New York winters.
He thought that playing golf and meeting new people would
help him adjust to his retirement. I was not keen on that idea,
still very devoted to my counseling work. I was not willing to
spend winters away, but agreed to take two week periods doing
phone sessions when out of town. I thought of a second home
as another place to take care of and there was nowhere that
particularly called me. For me the exploration was simply an
enjoyable chance to visit new destinations.

Bob began to do research that gave him purpose and energy.
Over the course of several years, we went to the east and west
coasts of Florida, and then to Santa Barbara and La Jolla in southern California. Going to lovely resorts on Long Boat Key, Palm
Beach, and Montecito was a pleasure, but I still wasn't interested
in a second home. As a last possibility Bob suggested Scottsdale,
Arizona. I had never been to the desert and was delighted to
investigate the idea further. Our first stop was the Camelback

Inn, near the base of Camelback Mountain. The mountain, like a giant sphinx, protects the sprawling, flat, sun-drenched plain. Its rough red texture is imposing, yet welcoming.

Shortly after arriving, I discovered a labyrinth set on church property in a natural desert at the foot of the mountain. Unlike the sandy Sahara, the Sonoran Desert is filled with life: trees, bushes, wild flowers, cactus, and animals. It was all new to me, exotic and beautiful to see but not to touch. The signs and sounds of modern life were close by, yet this open virgin space was a tranquil spot for a walking meditation. Winding safely through circling pathways with no concern of getting lost, I listened, as my thoughts became prayers when I reached the center. Standing in the heart of the labyrinth I looked around, saw and felt the power of Camelback Mountain, the beauty and variety of the desert, the quiet of nearby Mummy Mountain, and the ever-present blue sky. Filled with gratitude, I thought to myself, "This is my heaven."

Have you ever been somewhere that you knew you had been before, although you can't remember when? That is how the desert felt to me. I don't know about prior lifetimes; perhaps that was the source of my familiarity. It didn't matter. What did matter was that the desert filled my soul.

Our next stop was the Boulders, a resort in nearby Carefree. Just the name Carefree appealed to me. When I arrived, I immediately noticed the street names: Ho Road, Hum Road, Pleasant Place, Dream Street, Nonchalant Avenue, and Easy Street. Yes, it felt that way, too. The hotel was impressive, with an authentic emphasis on Native American culture and natural beauty. Driving past the bloom of a desert botanical garden, huge boulders were piled high, mountains were framed against vast azure skies unlike any I had ever seen other than in Egypt. The lobby was filled with handmade Native tapestries, baskets, and paintings.

We checked in and were brought to a lovely casita, appointed in tasteful southwest décor. I was immediately drawn outside to the sun, walking onto the small patio. Little white-tailed rabbits were hopping around, and a mother quail waddled toward me followed by her four babies. A cardinal was perched on a small bush, and a hummingbird hovered in space nearby. Tall stately saguaros stood with arms turned upward toward the heavens. The air was dry and clear, and the bright sun warmed my body. Bob stood quietly, watching me for a while. Then, smiling, he said, "I guess the Chamber of Commerce came out to meet you."

He was correct. I had immediately fallen in love with the desert. I said yes, I would give a second home a try, but with two terms. I would continue my work by phone during no more than two-week trips, and I would want to sell the house if it no longer felt good to me to be there. Bob readily accepted.

We quickly found a site and an architect and proceeded to build a beautiful home. It was stucco and glass with a full view of the mountains. Day after day we worked on it together, discussing plans and refining them to every last detail. We located landscape and lighting designers; we selected finishes, appliances, doorknobs, and light switches. Then into interior design: colors, furniture, carpets, and art. It was a joint creative process that was fun for me and enlivening and interesting to Bob. We were both thrilled with the house. Can you imagine waking up every morning to see nothing but rock covered mountains nearby and soft sloping ones in the distance, framed by vast, cloudless blue skies?

We spent part of the next three winters touring the great Southwest seeing the sights, learning about Native American art, music, culture, and spirituality. We bought art for our home, enjoyed spectacular nature, and traveled to the Navajo and Hopi reservations in Arizona and the Santa Clara reservation in New Mexico. We visited Santa Fe and Taos, and the awesome Grand Canyon and Bryce Canyon.

My favorite trips were to Sedona. It was a joy, passing through saguaro forests onto winding roads lined with cottonwood trees, coming around a bend to see the magnificence of Bell Rock. There were miles of deep red soil and towering red rocks, some of them representing familiar shapes: Cathedral Rock, Coffee Pot Rock, Chimney Rock, and Courthouse Butte. We took many trips there to hike trails and climb the rocks. We also learned about vortex energy and the medicinal value of plants.

It brought much sadness to visit the reservations and to see the disrespect that has befallen the Native peoples. The effects of mistreatment they endured at the hands of white settlers were evident. Their tribal nations have been reduced to small territories plagued with poverty, alcoholism, and obesity. Their main industry is gambling casinos and much of their youth have left home to join the outside culture. One day while at the Hopi reservation Bob and I stood on a bridge looking out at Second Mesa far in the distance. A native man approached me and, without invitation, said, "Be strong for yourself. Don't be strong for him. Don't be strong for them. Be strong for yourself. Do you see the blue sky, the white clouds, the red earth, the green plants and trees? All those colors are in you. That is what you are." I understood that he was referring to the energy chakras inside of us all. He waved his arms outward saying, "All of this is in you."

I still have his primitive calling card with his name and contact information. Someday I would like to visit him. It is strange how many years it took me to learn that I am connected to all that is, and that I first have to be strong for myself before I can be strong for others.

Once the house was completed and travel slowed down, life was again about everyday living. Bob sank back into his emptiness and depression. He had been distracted by the building project and trips but again found himself without a focus. Golf and social life did not provide the enjoyment he anticipated. He was still missing a sense of purpose, perhaps not even in our marriage. At times I believed that he wanted my attention more than the responsibility of resolving the obstacles to his happiness, but I dismissed that thought. It was too painful to accept.

One night I was lying in bed next to Bob, exhausted and discouraged by his continuing depression. I was as close to the edge of the bed as possible, separated from him by three feet, unable to sleep. My mind kept going back and forth, saying "no" and "yes." The "no" said, "I can't keep doing this. Bob doesn't make sense. I don't want to be near him. He is refusing to deal with the source his pain." The "yes" said, "Bob is suffering. I love him and support him. I want him to feel better."

After much deliberation, I finally chose "yes" and reached out my hand, not even my whole hand, just my fingertips. His unusually cool fingers immediately touched mine. He took my hand and we lay that way for quite a while, with his "yes" and his "no." His "yes" was: "I love her. Yes, I want to hold her." His "no": "I am not good to her, maybe not even good for her." After a while, as I turned over, away from him, he came behind me, spooned with my body, and we both fell asleep peacefully without saying a word. When love trumps pride, both partners win. Why was it so difficult to bridge those three feet, the distance of surrender? Why do I choose separation while longing to love, when love is what makes me happiest? What does it take to prioritize love?

Desiring to connect more with my spirit, I suggested that we go to a Christmas Eve service at Unity of Phoenix. I had not been to one in several years, and Bob had never been. Perhaps it would open both of our hearts.

Expecting a small country church, we were amazed to drive up to a large modern building that seated nine hundred people. A young, dynamic, and humorous minister led the service, directing congregants to look within to connect with their divine nature. He encouraged meditation and prayer to bring us closer to the divinity within us. The event ended with a candle-lighting ceremony. From the back row we saw one candle at a time growing into hundreds, slowly and softly lighting up the vast sanctuary.

Bob found the service uplifting. He was pleased with the message that God is within all of us, including him. He could easily relate to a loving God, not a punishing one. I was grateful to be at that service and pleased that Bob wanted to return. If he accepted a spirituality that resonated deeply within me, it could possibly bring us closer. Perhaps it could move us ahead in a sustainable positive direction. We continued to attend services each Sunday for the remainder of the winter.

That spring we decided to sell the Scottsdale house. We weren't using it enough to warrant the responsibility and expense. After living there five winters it was painful to see the precious desert being cut up into small parcels for homes and shopping malls, causing the coyotes and javelinas to move north to new habitats, and tall electric power lines to mar the expansive blue sky. On the last morning before leaving for the airport I drove to town and passed no fewer than eight cement trucks, noisily churning as they mixed material to lay new foundations. The magnitude of building in the area was tremendous. What was once peaceful desert was becoming a developed suburb.

The Arizona desert had changed dramatically, as had my marriage. Both were going through endings and new beginnings. Beautiful open desert landscapes had been cut into small separated fragments. Our marriage, once primarily vibrant and easy, was now cluttered with Bob's self-doubts and resistance to examining them. Lots of change, deaths and births, yet Scottsdale's future seemed much clearer to me than the direction of my marriage.

twenty nine

LIFE CYCLES

THE PHONE RANG. MY SISTER-IN-LAW WAS CRYING HYSTER-
ically: "Walt is dead, Walt is dead! I found him on the garage
floor. His finger marks slid down the side of the car, as if he was
trying to hold on before he collapsed. Walt is dead!"

My brother and his second wife Penny had moved to an
upscale golf community in Florida. His dream retirement from
his law firm had come true: a country club life of golf and social
connections. I had no idea that their living costs far exceeded
their resources. He had greatly surpassed our Dad's model of
spending beyond his means. It had come to the point that, at age
65, Walt was deeply in debt and was forced to go back to work. He
died as he returned home from a congratulatory dinner with his
new employer the evening before he was due to start his new job.

I was stunned and heartbroken. Although I knew Walt's
limitations, he was still my big brother. We were different personalities with contrasting values but we loved each other dearly.
I recalled the laughs we shared and the many places he took me.
I especially remember childhood trips to Ebbets Field to watch

the Brooklyn Dodgers and Jackie Robinson play baseball.

Walt's death left the burden of tending to my mother's needs squarely on my shoulders. Although I was sometimes annoyed that he didn't take on any of the responsibility for her care, he understood her well and was always there to listen to my difficulties with her and add some humor to the situation.

Mom was 91, becoming more frail daily. Her husband Mike died shortly after Walt, making it necessary for Bob and me to make frequent visits to Florida to deal with her declining physical and emotional condition. It weighed on my mind that I needed to tell her that Walt had passed. When I did she seemed unresponsive. Her eyes misted over but she never said a word about it. Never.

Mom was living at home with round the clock caregivers who, with no daily supervision, did little. On one trip I opened the refrigerator and found it empty except for one container of moldy Jell-O. On another, I was told that she had developed severe bedsores. Obviously she was not getting the care she needed and it was necessary to move her. Bob was especially generous in taking on the project of finding a first-rate assisted living facility.

We helped Mom move into a comfortable residence. At first she was happy with the attention, but within days became ill and was taken to the hospital by ambulance. She refused to eat, becoming gradually weaker. I stayed in Florida for ten more days but needed to return home for my work. I was in touch with her private nurse many times a day with plans to come back in two weeks. The nurse promised to let me know if Mom's condition worsened. How shocked I was when I received a call from her that Mom had died.

Although my primary feeling was relief, it was difficult to accept that it never was and never would be possible to have any satisfying intimacy with Mom. She was gone and that longing would never be met. Her passing would leave a big space in my life. Bob was present, helping with funeral arrangements and standing by me. I could always count on him when it came to family matters.

After my brother's and mother's deaths within a few months of each other, my daughter-in-law suggested that I look into the Option Institute in the Berkshires. The co-founders, "Bears" and Samarhia Kaufman, ran a center for families of autistic children and an adult program based on Bears' book: Happiness is A Choice. The title alone drew me.

Bob and I agreed to immerse ourselves in an 8-week program in Massachusetts the following year. The core of the course was examining beliefs, sorting out those that served to expand our lives and happiness and those that diminish our self-esteem and opportunities. They taught that beliefs create feelings, which in turn create decisions and actions. We were encouraged to be kind to ourselves and others, realizing that we always do our best, given our beliefs at the time, and that beliefs can be changed. Our stay was filled with insights, friendship, fun and challenge.

A day that stands out was when I stood at the edge of a chasm. A deep valley separated me from a mountain across the way. I shouted "hello" and received my "hello" back. I was surprised, so I began to play: "This is fun" came echoing back. "You are beautiful." How good that felt. "I love you." Could I begin to say that to myself without an echo? That day was the beginning of my understanding that the energy I am sending out gets reflected back to me. That realization had enormous impact.

Bob's mother died within months of the end of the program. A few years later Bob's son Ken, age 43, was diagnosed with pancreatic cancer, a fatal illness. Bob and Ken were not close and tension between them was obvious. I spent two years emotionally supporting Bob, Ken and his family, making frequent phone calls and visits to Texas. It was a consuming and heartbreaking time, watching Ken wasting away, going through his illness and death before our eyes.

Ken's death was a relief for both Bob and me. I think, by that time, for his wife Suzanne, as well. I couldn't tell how it was for his two daughters, aged four and six. They were quite stoic. Ken's intense suffering was unbearable to watch. Suzanne kept her promise to him that he would die at home, as the children faced the pain of their father's decline day after day. Bob and I were united in our support for Suzanne to move him to hospice when he lost consciousness. He died the next day.

I was glad to go to Arizona and have some peace. Bob, who was most appreciative of my presence through this prolonged painful time, was attentive and considerate. Slowly, he began to think about ways to bring some lightness into our lives: he brought flowers home, suggested beautiful dinners and lovely walks in the desert. They were comforting yet for months after, there was still no intimacy. It almost felt like Bob's life force had died, as he went through the motions, nice motions, yet lifeless.

Exhausted by Ken's illness and death and the unhappiness that preceded it, I was utterly drained. Something had changed within me. I told Bob that I could no longer bear the burden of so much unhappiness; extreme family issues and loss coupled with an absence of intimacy in our marriage. I was willing to be there in the difficult times that show up in life, but those times cannot be all times. I needed to laugh and play, dance and relax. I needed heart connection. I needed to receive. I needed happiness. I was no longer willing to give away my life and my energy. Looking through my rose-colored glasses, insisting that all would somehow work out well had been my stubbornness, loving neither to Bob nor myself.

For the first time I realized that despite Bob's repeated words, he did not share my dream of partnership. My dream was so clear to me, every facet of it: two people grounded in pleasure, giving and receiving, separate and connected, each open to and sharing their creativity and emotional, sexual and spiritual feelings. Man and woman in authentic relationship, centered and content in their own lives on a journey towards unconditional love.

That dream was mine alone and I could not require Bob to fit into it. I had been certain that since he obviously loved me, we wanted the same dream. After all, it is a beautiful dream, although I had not restated it clearly since our honeymoon, twenty years earlier.

Bob's dream showed up differently. In it he was loved, received much attention and was elevated and enlivened by my presence. He wanted to feel safe and comfortable, unchallenged, with little risk. His dream included beautiful homes, worldly adventures together, supporting me with my family and giving me anything I wanted in the material world. He expressed his love with romantic sentimentality, believing that sending flowers, cards, love letters and gifts would fill me.

Stopped dead in my tracks, I began to think about my dream, so different from his. His was a fine dream, but it did not meet my soul. My tears flowed as I realized why I was unhappy. Dreams are our own; a vision of what each of us desires to create in our life. I knew that I would hold onto my dream without reservation, without wavering. It might mean that Bob would step up and meet it. It might mean that I would need to let go of him to make space to fulfill mine. I was clear that Bob could never meet my dream unless it became his.

With some promising moments and despite many disappointments, I still held hope for deep soul partnership with Bob. Struggling with a severely diminished libido, I did not know whether our marriage could be reignited. For many years we had enjoyed family times, travel, social life, compatible tastes and sensibilities, in addition to work challenges, but the fire was out.

I decided that while it would be difficult for me, I would just allow events to unfold. The direction of the relationship would become clear to both of us. I was not sure whether it was dying or slowly moving into a new incarnation. Bob would either address the barriers to his happiness or remain in avoidance. I realized that there was a real possibility that he would not make a different choice and I might have to move on.

I did not want to go through divorce, no, not again. It would feel so painful, even shameful. My first divorce had been a soul-selfish step, my birth as a self-loving woman able to contribute in ways I had never dreamed possible. My dependent good girl had grown-up. I was finally present and visible, first of all to myself. My prayer was that Bob would find his way back to love and pleasure and share that with me. I felt surprisingly calm and safe, certain that I would move towards my soul's happiness no matter what. It was Bob's decision whether to join me.

From that place of surrender I put my attention on self-care as my new beginning. I would stand more firmly in what I valued and wanted. After giving unending support and dealing with so much death, I was ready for life! My inner voice was shouting: "Enough, I am done! I want a vibrant life filled with joy. I alone choose my direction. I am no longer the girl or woman who gives and gives at all costs, requiring little for myself. I want to love and be loved."

Unconditional love was my deepest longing. Could I begin with myself? At times I well up remembering my faithful little Yorkie Clyde. He was fierce with others yet always tender with me. After my divorce he often sat on my pillow licking away my tears as I lay on my bed crying. When he became too feeble to function I was with him in the vet's office as he trustingly stood on the examining table. One of my hands supported his warm chest as I felt his last heart beats; the other was on his back. The vet injected him with a solution of mercy and I felt him yield into my hand and pass on. I had never experienced that level of peace before.

Endings are an intrinsic part of the life cycle leading to new beginnings. My divorce and all these deaths showed me that there is always pain in loss, even when accompanied by relief. I also learned that after sufficient grief has been released, mourning does end. Change continues. It always will. Life brightens again.

thirty

MAMA GENA

IN SUMMER 2006, I ATTENDED A UNITY CHURCH RETREAT.
Class time was filled with lectures, exercises, meditation, and
music. Daily hour-long, small connection groups were set up to
share our thoughts about class content and provide a safe space
to voice personal issues. I focused on my desire to create more
intimacy in my marriage.

Five of the six people in my group were long-standing congregants. A woman, new to Unity, was quite skeptical. I noticed
her because she always wore very feminine sundresses in this
casual setting. She was attractive with long, pretty hair, and she
listened intently to all of us but rarely shared in the group. I
admired her authenticity as she was open in her questions and
communicated what she didn't accept. On the last day of the
retreat she offered me a small, tidily wrapped gift. Her card read,
"Just another perspective."

She said, "I have been listening to you and think you might
be interested in reading this. It's a bit over the top, but I think
you will like it." I was surprised and pleased, thanked her for

thinking of me, and took her name and contact information so that I could respond.

Her gift was Regena Thomashauer's book *Mama Gena's School of Womanly Arts*. The tag line was "Using the Power of Pleasure to Have Your Way in the World." I took it home and put it on my night table but didn't pick it up for ten months. When I finally started it, I read it voraciously. It hit me like a bolt of lightning. Who am I as a *woman*, not a mother, wife, friend, daughter, or sister? Who am I as a woman? I didn't know how to answer that question.

I put down the book, feeling unsettled and anxious. An incident that happened more than forty years earlier came to mind. I was at Raffles, an "in" Los Angeles nightspot with my husband Werner and another couple, who were his old college friends. The place was aglow, the atmosphere festive and celebratory. Glasses clinked with toasts and the room was filled with laughter and music.

When we were settled, I took in the scene and noticed Shirley MacLaine sitting at a large table nearby. She was stunning, her red hair shining, wearing an off-the-shoulder emerald green satin dress. Her sparkling eyes and earrings glistened, and her smile lit up the room. She looked sexy, radiant, and captivating. I sat at our table of four feeling dwarfed by her presence, envious of her beauty and magnetism. I was wearing a conservative simple gray knit sheath, listening to conversation about the stock market that bored me yet not knowing how to redirect it. I felt dull and helpless. I was two years younger than Shirley but the gap between us was a chasm, a distance I did not know how to navigate. I was out of my league and comfort zone, far away from my four children, feeling small, sad, and sexless. The grayness of my dress and emotion were in sharp contrast to her luminous presence. A deep sense of failure overtook me, and I wanted to go home to my children where I felt safe. Yet there I was, feeling very much like "Plain Jane."

Four decades had passed since I saw the memorably dazzling Shirley MacLaine and I still felt incomplete as a woman. When I picked up Mama Gena's book again and thought about what I wanted in my life, it brought tears to my eyes. Although I saw myself as loving, effective, and intelligent I also wanted to feel beautiful, sexy, playful, and radiant. The next morning, I decided to enroll in the Mastery program of the School of Womanly Arts.

I was excited to attend my first class in Manhattan. The theater was large, seating more than two-hundred women in comfortable, red velvet chairs. Pink feather boas were everywhere, draped around stairway banisters and aisle seats and along the rim of the large well-lit stage. A tall director's chair and table with a huge vase filled with beautiful pink roses drew my attention.

I was happy to be there, comfortable even though I didn't know anyone. Each woman was given a nametag with the prefix SG, an abbreviation for Sister Goddess. I was SG Jane and I sat next to SG Sarah. I asked why we are called Sister Goddesses and learned that we are sisters to one another and are goddesses because we are connected to the Divine. As seats began to fill there was an excited buzz in the room. Before long, Mama Gena came onto the stage dressed in a high-fashion, form-fitting outfit. Her arms were outstretched to embrace us all as she said dramatically: "Have no fear, Mama Gena is here."

She was vibrant, brilliant, saucy, and free. After welcoming us, she immediately asked us to share "brags," incidents that made us feel proud. Responding spontaneously, she expanded them with compelling comments that were insightful, bold, funny, and loving. It felt good to be there, listening to these success stories, yet I didn't choose to share.

Mama Gena sat on the edge of the stage and began to talk about the patriarchy that has existed for thousands of years, and how it has affected us as women. She called the effects "invisible chains." She spoke about how we are seen and how we see ourselves, emphasizing that we habitually take on the expected role of nurturing everyone around us while neglecting ourselves. She reminded us that we are often minimized, disconnected from our beauty and the fuel of our sexuality. Until recent times women had lost the value of femininity and the critical importance of our bond with each other, often living in isolation and quiet despair. I felt like she was describing me personally. She explained her vision of community: women standing together for the purpose of creating and sharing pleasure and fulfilling our dreams. It was clear that she deeply loved women and wanted every single one of us to blossom.

Mama Gena encouraged us to choose on behalf of our desires rather than the demands of others or our historic internalized "shoulds." She encouraged us to decide according to our appetite instead of giving away our energy to meet cultural expectations. It was a challenging shift given my ingrained habit of serving others first, often with the consequence of feeling depleted and diminished.

Mama Gena then talked about the beauty and sacredness of our sexuality. As she spoke slowly and gently, with such sensitivity and love, I was able to relax and receive her words. She told us that our bodies are beautiful masterpieces to be adored and worshipped.

I cried for most of that morning as she repeatedly urged woman after woman to embrace her full sexual body. I was not the only woman crying. Almost everyone was, for each of us had diminished our sexual connection. My tears were about decades of shame, neglect, and disregard. They kept coming in a soft, unending stream that I thought would never end. The pain of my old beliefs and sexual history was excruciating. Never had my parents, boyfriends, husbands—or I—deeply valued or appreciated my femininity. I had held my sexuality as dark and dangerous; now Mama Gena introduced it as a sacred part of myself to be honored.

Can you imagine two hundred women mourning their own and others' disrespect of their holy bodies? The shared grief in the room was colossal. Women of all ages, appearances, and backgrounds supported each other in their pain, bonding on a level I had never before shared with even my closest friends. It was the most holy space I had ever known. Mama Gena's reverence for feminine sexuality and the support of the entire group touched my soul.

After that session I had an introductory lunch with six classmates. We would be a pod that stayed together throughout the course. My mind was still back in the Mastery room, and I was pleased that we talked openly about the powerful events of the morning. As it turned out, two of my dearest friends today sat at that table with me.

The afternoon session was much lighter, with intermittent music called dance-breaks. I watched the young woman sitting in front of mine dance joyfully and gracefully, her long auburn hair flowing easily as she moved. I felt stiff, awkward, and jealous. She was a Big Sister, and I hoped that someday I would be able to dance like that too.

By the end of the day I was a changed woman, feeling excited, open-hearted, and outgoing. My whole body felt alive. Happily raising my hand, I took the microphone and shared my day's journey with these two hundred women, new friends who already felt like sisters. I had gone through my deepest healing, releasing the agony of verbal abuse and the dishonoring of my sexuality. Miraculously I was able to embrace the beauty of my body with pride and pleasure. I arrived home, overflowing with warmth, love, and turn-on that pleased my husband Bob.

I was skeptical of many radical ideas that Mama Gena

presented in future classes. One notion was that men love to serve women. That was not my life experience, in fact quite the opposite. She taught that since women are usually more connected to their emotional, sensual, and spiritual feelings, we must lead the way with our desires. Men, although not realizing it, need women's leadership to feel successful with us.

I decided to give these ideas a try. After all, what was there to lose? My attempt to support Bob in dealing with his problems wasn't working. Mama Gena recommended that I take my focus off my marriage and put it on myself for a year. She suggested that I invest in my pleasure, keep myself happy, and bring that to my husband and everyone else in my life. I could invite Bob to join me when I wanted, always staying committed to my direction whether or not he accepted my invitations. My first priority was to satisfy myself. My husband, children, friends, and communities would certainly benefit as a result.

I began to fill myself, planning something to look forward to each day. Bob soon joined me in many playful activities. I arranged tennis dates and parties, dancing, and shopping trips. He was responsive, and it made a huge difference in the quality of my days and the connection in our marriage. Clearly he wanted to spend time with me and our relationship began to be based more on my pleasurable terms than on his problems, a win for both of us. I was creating intimacy through pleasure and receiving Bob's contributions with appreciation. He began to suggest movies, shows, and concerts that I received with enthusiasm. My excited responses to Bob's initiatives pleased him and motivated him to create more. We were on an upward spiral. Mama Gena's advice proved to be extremely wise. Grateful women make men feel like heroes.

I have long believed that we live in a world where our energy attracts its likeness. My unhappiness and anger had attracted more of the same, and my pleasure in feeling beautiful, sensual, and joyful did, too. Still it surprised me to see how easily I fell back into prioritizing Bob's needs, and how often he drew on my attention through sharing problems rather than initiating pleasures. Yes, the patriarchy also affects men.

Mama Gena repeatedly emphasized the importance of reclaiming and deepening our sensuality. Her comfort with her own encouraged us to honor and treasure ours. She promised that it would transform our lives, since it is the source of our radiance and life force. Given my history, I was in extremely delicate territory, but I eagerly took the plunge to connect with and love my whole body.

I learned that men and women commonly do not understand that to make a relationship work, a woman's sensual pleasure has to be both partners' priority. If not, as time goes by, women frequently lose turn-on and interest, feigning fatigue and head-aches to avoid sexual encounters. Slowly, slowly the energy ebbs between the two, and neither really knows why. Arguments arise about work, money, children, and in-laws while this core issue remains unaddressed and unresolved. Through time, pas-sionless relationships end in grief, resentment or betrayal, or remain intact in distance or deadness. I did not want that to happen again.

The Sister Goddess community was a blessing to me. I looked forward to the School of Womanly Arts events, which were filled with laughter, tears, courage, dance, connection, fun, and growth. Women purged their grief in the arms of other women and shared their victories to the delight of their sisters. Women claimed their beauty with the support of other women and met their fears in the safety of the group. I always came home from classes feeling vibrant and full. We were all feeling more beau-tiful, joyful, and sexy month by month.

It has been many years since I attended Mastery, and I fol-lowed with advanced courses at the School of Womanly Arts.

What I learned there continues to enhance my life. Instead of burying my pain, fear, and frustration, I now use the tools I learned to empty those feelings safely within the community. When I fall back into old patterns I lean in and call on Sister Goddesses for support.

How different my life would have been had I known long ago who I was as a woman. How strong I would have felt knowing that my pleasure was primary. How different I would have felt standing for my sensuality rather than feeling resentful that my husbands were neglecting it. How beautiful I would have felt regardless of their choices.

Mama Gena is the womb that held and nourished me in my early seventies, birthing me into my full womanhood. Her vision and tireless passion changed my life. After dozens of years of self-study, I learned to love my femininity, the core that unified all my other self-realizations. I felt whole. My bonds with Sister Goddesses have deepened through the years and the sisterhood continues to stand with me, as together we move toward fulfilling our desires. I now proudly claim that pleasure is my daily focus.

thirty one

SEXUALITY: LATE BLOOMER

I GREW UP IN A TIME WHEN SEX WAS NOT A VISIBLE PART OF life, not even in the movies. The culture encouraged motherhood and nurturing while undervaluing it, and either hid or shamed feminine sexuality.

When I entered adolescence, I was blessed with a shapely body and vibrant sexuality that created a shockwave in my family. It frightened my father who attempted to extinguish it. It added to my obese mother's shame and self-rejection. My four-year-older brother, inappropriately attracted to me, was jealous of my boyfriends. Family dynamics, cultural taboos, and the fear that my sexual feelings would lead me to disgrace created huge shame, limiting my sexual exploration. I felt a deep divide within. My blooming sexuality yearned for experience while the pain of repression nagged.

Through my entire first marriage and during the middle years of my second, sex was unsatisfying. I kept my body healthy and attractive, yet felt a continual unmet longing. Despite the positive value that each marriage offered, my sexual desires remained unfulfilled.

The psychologist Carl Jung taught that there are two aspects of femininity: maternal-nurturing and sexual-creative. I moved toward maternal-nurturing. It felt safer. Three sons and a daughter filled my life, all brilliant, interesting, attractive, and high-spirited. They brought purpose, laughter, happiness, and love to my daily experience.

It was the sexual part that was problematic. Essentially, my first marriage felt parental. The dominance of my nurturing self over my sexual self attracted a man who drew from it. Werner, while handsome, smart, and extremely able professionally, was emotionally immature and focused mainly on his needs, his wants, and his stardom. We both made his desires our priority for more than thirteen years. When I began to ask, "What about me?" the marriage began to disintegrate. These attitudes pervaded our sexual life as well as our family and worldly experience and led to our divorce.

After my separation I began a relationship with Ron, a considerably younger man. I was forty, and it was the first time I'd had a satisfying sex life. I stayed involved with him for ten years while I took care of my children and established my career. We were helpmates for each other with no desire or pressure for more commitment. I knew he would never be my life partner, which suited me well until I began to desire one. When that time came, my old friend Bob, a recent widower, reentered my life.

From the beginning I was excited about Bob, yet concerned about ending my relationship with Ron. Since I believed that Ron was responsible for my sexual pleasure, it was hard to leave him. Despite my concern, I had to move on as I deeply desired and was ready to invest in a full, satisfying peer partnership on all levels. My relationship with Bob developed quickly and happily, and we were married a year later.

In the beginning our sex life was fun and experimental. I was surprised at how free I was and how easily I shared my experience with him. Bob was delighted. Sadly, this changed dramatically when he encountered severe business setbacks that had a deep emotional impact on him. He was depressed and found it difficult to focus on any pleasures.

Years later, while enrolled in Mama Gena's school, I learned that my turn-on is my responsibility, that I create my own rapturous sexual feelings. I can do that in my mind in fantasy, when alone, while noticing an attractive man, or with a partner. She taught that it is for me to know my body, know what pleases me, and to communicate how I want to be touched, pleasured, and loved. She said that it is completely my choice to allow my feelings to flow, and that a man can only activate my sensations to the degree that I let myself feel them.

Once I accepted the truth that my pleasure originates with me, I wanted to know more. I had significantly deepened my emotional and spiritual life, and I wanted to expand my sensual and sexual capacities. Although my sex life with Ron had been gratifying, lingering self-doubt from Werner's ongoing infidelity still pained me. One of my teachers explained that unless a woman trusts her partner she will not be able to surrender to her deeper sexuality. Trust was such a major issue in my first marriage, and her explanation eased my sexual insecurity.

I also accepted the Indian master Bhagwan Rajneesh's teachings. He said that until sex is fully experienced as a natural and beautiful part of a person's life, spiritual development will continually be hampered. I was excited to pursue a path where my body and soul, sexuality, and divinity were joined. I often wonder why, in churches and synagogues, there is silence about sexuality. Isn't the pleasure of sex sacred? Can we ever fully know ourselves while denying our sexual nature?

Desiring to awaken to my wholeness, I began a daily practice focusing on my senses, noticing simple, everyday sensual pleasures. How lovely it felt when the air gently caressed my skin while driving my car. Listening to Pavarotti sing arias from *La Bohème* filled my heart. Dancing the Argentine tango, doing ochos and flicks, called forth my gracefulness. The touch of my husband's lips softly meeting mine created tingles that streamed through my body. My sensual responses were immediate and involuntary, creating feelings of aliveness that connected me to my spirit.

As I became more sensually attuned I began to address my sexual life. What would enrich my enjoyment and enhance my partner's? I chose sensitive healers and respectful teachers who encouraged me to let go of painful past memories stored in my mind and body and taught techniques that opened me to greater pleasure.

Surprisingly I found that expanding sexuality was like learning anything else. It took unwavering desire and commitment, knowledge, and practice to grow my own pleasure capacity. Realizing that I was neither dependent upon nor subject to a partner's sexual experience dramatically changed my belief that I needed a man, replacing it with the desire for one.

Sharing these experiences with Bob was a delicate process, for men in our generation (and perhaps still today) were taught to believe that they "know" and are "in charge." Yet, how can a man know a woman as well as she knows herself? As Bob began to accept that idea, he was more at ease. Sexual pleasure deepened our intimacy and overflowed into our daily lives.

I am forever grateful that I listened to the nagging of my sexual desire, never giving up on expressing it. It had been my most painful loss, the most challenging chapter of my soul selfish journey. Standing for my soul living inside my yearning body, I reclaimed my sexual wholeness. In intimate moments I know they are one. Like a flower with its roots watered by a sustaining life force, my physical body is connected to my emotions, my heart, and my soul.

Reclaiming my sexual openness enhanced my feelings of beauty and pride in being a woman. As I began to feel more beautiful I gradually changed my outer appearance: style, colors, hair-do, body posture, and movement. I now often receive compliments about my attractiveness, elegance and grace, which echo these new feelings.

Remarkably, there was another unexpected outcome. I became an inspiration to many women in their 40s, 50s and 60s in the Sister Goddess community. In their minds they were living on a countdown, worried about aging and decline. My transformation reassured them, giving them the belief that they could have decades of growth and radiance ahead.

It makes me happy to model agelessness to women decades younger. My life demonstrates that looking within and going deeper into the realms of emotional, sexual, and spiritual feeling creates freedom. The loss of youth and even middle age no longer need to determine a woman's beauty and vibrancy. It is now real to me that a woman of 80 can still feel attractive and alive if she stays connected to her emotions, her sexuality, and her authentic self, her soul.

I don't live on a countdown. My intention is to maintain my radiance, however long I am on this planet.

thirty two

FORGIVENESS

MY CHILDREN WERE ALARMED. THEIR FATHER, NOW 66, WAS diagnosed with endocarditis, a serious infection in the inside lining of the heart chambers. He was rushed to the hospital and put on around-the-clock antibiotics to quell it. The danger was that the infectious "vegetation" in his heart might break off and flow to his brain causing a stroke.

How could this happen to such a vibrant man? Werner had a mitral valve issue and for years had been required to take antibiotics before dental cleanings. This time he had not done so.

After a few days I was told that he was recovering well, and I deliberated about whether to visit him. I had not seen him for quite some time, working with myself to let go of the pain of our divorce and his choices that followed. I knew I had to release my resentments to move ahead. It would benefit me to let go of my anger and victimhood even though he had severely punished me financially and undermined many of my parental decisions.

Therapy taught me that releasing blame would free me, perhaps free both of us. Like a hook, blame kept me emotionally attached to Werner. I understood the concept, but it took me some time to be willing to embrace it. Even though I felt entitled to my righteous anger, his illness was a real crisis, a time to let go of the past. I felt like a heroine when I thought about visiting him in goodwill and decided I would. Still, I was also clear that I did not want to open the door to any ongoing relationship.

On the way to the hospital I stopped to buy him some cookies and pastries, recalling how much of a sweet tooth he had. I was surprised that I enjoyed selecting these gifts and entered the hospital relaxed and happy.

As soon as I walked into his room I was relieved to see him looking as vital and energetic as I remembered. His blue eyes shining, he was obviously happy to see me and received my presents and presence with appreciation.

Then he began to talk, pretty much dominating the conversation, an all too familiar experience. The difference was that now he was repeating himself. From time to time he would say the same sentence, with the same intonation, apparently having no idea that he had just said it. I was familiar with that kind of repetition since my mother-in-law often similarly repeated herself as a result of several mini-strokes. I was shocked. The children had spoken about the danger of a stroke but had not mentioned that he'd had one. It was disorienting to be with him, spirited, looking well, yet so altered.

Our visit ended with warm feelings that pleased me. It was a major triumph to visit and support him and feel genuine compassion. In fact, I felt heartbroken. It was difficult to accept that his brilliant mind seemed to have been irreparably damaged.

Days later my daughter Susan asked if I would go with her to visit her Dad. Just like when she was ten years old, I accompanied her so that she would feel safe. When we got there we found him unconscious, slumped over in a chair, in a treatment room by himself. We immediately called for help. This time Werner had suffered a severe stroke. I was grateful that Susan wasn't there alone.

This stroke left him with major short-term memory loss. He was confused about who people were, thinking our grandson was one of our sons. His long-term memory was intact. Werner could still speak fluent German, the language of his childhood, and he clearly remembered incidents from decades earlier.

Once again I was faced with old feelings about this man. Not only had he punished me, he now had suffered serious damage himself and caused my children great pain. It was difficult not to blame him for ignoring his medical instructions. I was in a dilemma. Years ago, I had freed myself from living with Werner with great difficulty. It was now time to liberate myself emotionally. I wanted to support my children through their ordeal but would not allow myself to be enmeshed in his health crisis or its consequences.

Letting go of my blame would require forgiveness. There was no middle ground. I began to ask: "What is forgiveness?" Was it a pardon—I, in my generosity, choose to forgive your wrongdoing? As the judge of right or wrong, do I decide on your penalty or freedom? That gave me a false sense of power but not release. It was the opposite of freedom, binding me to my unhappy experience.

A friend of mine suggested I join her Course in Miracles group that deals with forgiveness. I knew nothing about the Course and found it challenging and difficult. It teaches that, without exception, every action is either a call for love or an expression of love. Fear is seen as the opposite of love. Forgiveness is simply a letting go of past grievances in order to maintain a peaceful and loving inner state. Holding on to grievances prevents us from experiencing peace. Rather than judging what I saw as wrong, could I choose forgiveness for the benefit of all?

It seemed impossible to let go of Werner's harmful choices. Yet did I want to live my life weighed down by my judgments about him? I soon realized that it was my thoughts about Werner—not Werner—that weighed me down. The few moments of compassion I felt for him encouraged me to see that his choices need not continue to deplete me. I did not have to condone them, but I needed to let go of them to open myself to a more peaceful and joyful life.

Redefining forgiveness and attempting to accept Werner's behavior brought me to think about forgiving myself. I knew that my decision to end our marriage had caused all six of us great pain. Perhaps I could ask my children for their forgiveness. If I could think of the divorce simply as what I believed was best for my children and me, I could release the blame I held against myself all these years. I could focus on designing a happier life. I could let Werner's choices be. They were no longer part of my life.

I began to see that even the most difficult challenges offer benefits. Pain, just like joy, can be used for expansion. If I had not left Werner and suffered such major financial consequences, it would not have been necessary to muster the drive and energy to create my professional life. I would not have connected to my strength or discovered my gifts to share in service. Nor would I have reclaimed my womanhood, or created the possibility of a happy intimate relationship. Can I see my experiences as useful, regardless of my immediate happiness or sadness? Can I look for the value in every situation? Can I let us all off the hook, free from my judgments?

It was time to be more generous to all of us: myself, Werner, my brother, and our parents, to accept that we do the best we can, given our beliefs at the time. I found that forgiveness is kindness—kindness to myself and to others. It released me from the arrogance of righteousness and victimhood, from feeling entitled to and superior in my grievances. It put me in contact with my humility, accepting that we all make errors and have vulnerabilities. I experienced forgiveness as a sweet expression of soul selfishness, creating more inner peace and happier connection with others.

Werner spent the rest of his life in a nursing home, not knowing where he was, physically healthy but mentally unable to function. He died at seventy-two. I was surprised that I had no emotional response when he passed. Werner had died within me long before.

t h i r t y   t h r e e

REFLECTIONS
ON MOM

AS I FELT THE BENEFITS OF FORGIVING WERNER, I BEGAN TO
look at other grievances and judgments I was holding. Mom was
at the top of my list. Could I find my way to forgive her, too?
That would require me to mourn the losses of my childhood
and let them go. Holding onto my resentment to Mom kept
them in place.

Mom passed in February 1998 at the age of ninety-one. I felt
some ambivalence but primarily relief. I was glad that she was at
peace and that my decades of caretaking had ended. The years
of dealing with her unhappiness and tending to her needs had
been extremely draining and were finally over.

I have often wondered about that deep look in Mom's eyes
the day of my last visit. She asked me to tell her about the happy
times I remembered with her. I had a sinking feeling inside, not
knowing what to say. I told her I was grateful for her gentleness,
so unlike her mother. I told her that I appreciated her visiting

me in Texas soon after I got married, and later in Idaho when I was pregnant, and how I felt her concern for me. I wished I could have been more generous.

For several months after Mom died, I was upset that the nurse had not called me sooner. I was due to return in two weeks and asked the nurse to call if Mom's condition worsened. Maybe Mom told her not to call. Didn't she want me there? Didn't she want to say "good-bye" or "I love you," or give me the chance to say something more? Was Mom saying good-bye on my last visit, even though I didn't know it? Perhaps that was the look in her eyes that I didn't understand.

As years passed I still thought about Mom with sadness. She was a needy woman starving for love, yet she was never filled no matter how much she received. As a child she was emotionally abused, often criticized and punished. As a mother she was incapable of giving much. It used to anger me when neighbors told me what a lovely mother I had. She did not demand from them what she did from Dad and me, relying on us to fill her emptiness. Even though Mom told me she had longed for a girl after Walt was born, I think she wanted a good mother far more. For how can a woman who is still a sad, unhappy child be a nurturing mother?

Mom's life was primarily in reaction to her mother. Mine was too. Yet when I consider Mom's life separate from me, I see hers was harder, as she was subject to Baba's mean and unreasonable whims daily. She was certainly a sensitive and kind child, and I can't imagine what it must have been like for her. Perhaps longing for mother connection is so primal that children, no matter how old, never get over it. Perhaps it is a loss too great to bear.

The only happy photos I saw of Mom were those taken when she was a legal stenographer before she married. She enjoyed working and looked energized and confident. I think that is how she met my Dad, while working for another lawyer. Mom worked before Walt was born and in Dad's office beginning when I was a junior in high school. Those days were her best years. Her happiness was always away from home. Through the years of my inner journey, I learned that a woman's childhood pain is often reactivated when she becomes a mother. Perhaps mothering our own children unconsciously brings us back to our conflicts with our own mothers.

I remember sitting next to Mom at Baba's funeral. I couldn't understand why she was weeping bitterly. The rabbi, a stranger to the family, was speaking about Baba being a good woman. The eulogy was so ludicrous that Walt and I started laughing, unable to contain ourselves. During my last pregnancy, Mom asked me to name my baby after Baba if I had a girl. I said, "No!" How could she possibly ask that of me? Because she was so insistent, I agreed to use Baba's initial in my daughter's middle name.

When Dad was dying, Mom would not leave him for a moment. She stayed in his hospital room day and night while he was in a coma, and she was with him when he passed. Mom loved Dad deeply, depended on him enormously, and couldn't conceive of life without him. She was so depressed throughout his illness that she couldn't eat, losing more than 100 pounds. She looked like a totally different woman. Mom was hysterical at Dad's funeral, crying uncontrollably. Several people approached me, asking me to take care of her, showing no concern for my loss. It felt similar to my experience at Aunt Rose's funeral when I was ten. Dad and Aunt Rose, both devoted and kind, were Mom's loved ones. Hopefully my brother and I were too.

My Aunt Tillie, Mom's sister-in-law, stayed with her for a few days after Dad's funeral. Mom was not capable of living alone, isolated in a New York City apartment. Walt and I finally convinced her to move to Florida where Aunt Tillie lived, with many friends and activities in her building. Mom didn't care where she lived. In fact she said she didn't want to live, but after a while she agreed to move. I made the arrangements and Walt and I took her on the plane, one on each arm. The three of us went shopping to buy what she needed to set up her apartment. She was so numb that she couldn't make a decision, not even about a toaster. It was scary to leave her, but Aunt Tillie promised she would check in on her daily and keep us posted.

Miraculously, within a month, Mom made friends. A male neighbor accompanied her to help her buy a car. She befriended a handicapped young man at the pool, attracted to him as she was to all people in pain. Eventually he introduced her to his father who was a widower and they started dating. Within months, Mom called to tell me that she was getting married!

Her happiness with her new husband Mike did not last long. She began to put on weight, eventually regaining what she had lost. In a short time Mom began to complain that Mike was forceful, arrogant, and controlling. Although he did everything for her like my Dad did, he wasn't a good Dad. He was more like her bad Mom. It seemed like all the venomous childhood anger that she had repressed toward her cruel mother came out at him. She put no brakes on pouring out her harsh rage. I think that was the way her mother must have been to her. It was ugly to be around Mom and Mike.

The truth is that all the women in our family were unhappy. Baba was mean and angry, Mom was depressed and helpless, Aunt Rose was doing her best to escape, and I was sad and invisible behind my "good girl" mask. Who knows how many unhappy generations of un-mothered mothers there were in our lineage. I decided that if I were going to break the chain of my troubled history, I needed to let go of my grievances. I needed to forgive Mom.

My first step was to let myself feel my buried pain, anger, and resentment. Challenging as that was, the emotional release slowly opened space, allowing me to more deeply grasp what Mom's life had been. I began to feel compassion for her, seeing her as a hurt child living in a woman's body. How fortunate that she married Dad, whose pleasure it was to care for her.

I began to see that the degree of unhappiness and dependency Mom modeled was exactly the fuel that ignited me to continually seek and find as much of my authentic self as I have. I wanted to feel more love and peace, it was time to be kinder and focus on her positive qualities. I found many.

Mom was appreciative of what people gave her, often asking for more, yet always grateful. She resonated with others' suffering and possessed unusual empathy. I inherited her ability to receive, genuinely appreciating gifts and kind attention. Her qualities of loyalty, perceptive listening, intuition, and sensitivity also live in me, serving me well personally and professionally. It makes me happy to feel gratitude to her and finally be able to say, "Thanks for these priceless gifts, Mom."

To this day, what makes me most grateful was Mom's willingness to share me with my Aunt Rose. I wondered why she did that so freely. Was it for Aunt Rose, who wanted a child more than anything? Was it for me to have more mothering than she was capable of giving? Was it to relieve herself? Whatever her motivation, she gave me access to love and attention she couldn't give. I received it more happily than anything else in my childhood. Mom was never jealous of the love between me and Aunt Rose. In fact, she encouraged it, happy that we were so close. Maybe Mom saw me as a treasure, a jewel. Perhaps since she and Aunt Rose lived in their misery together, she wanted to share her blessing. Perhaps I was that joy!

I could never have come to this tender place had I not taken my soul selfish journey. How much lighter I feel. Mom did her best by just being gentle—absent but mercifully gentle. I wish I could have given her more acknowledgment. I wish I could have been forgiving while she was alive. It has taken me a long time and much prodding.

Mom never took such a journey. In fact, she died with her pain. I hope my forgiveness is a kindness to both of us. Thinking of her as a spirit, unencumbered by her emotional pain and awkward, heavy body, I see her free and with Dad, where she always wanted to be. I hope so, and that she will be eternally happy.

thirty four

SEVENTY-FIFTH BIRTHDAY PARTY

WHEN I WAS FIVE I DREAMED OF PRINCESS PARTIES WEARING tiaras, flared lacy pink dresses and shiny Mary Jane black patent leather shoes. I loved to dance and wanted to wear colorful costumes and play with glitter. That never happened at my home. I waited another seventy years to have the party of my dreams and was then given one fit for a queen.

My only childhood birthday party was when I was eight. Mom prepared a luncheon on her own, which made me feel special. I sat in the middle of an oblong table with seven friends, both boys and girls, feeling happy to have them in my home. They were rarely there since I was afraid to invite them, worried that Baba would be mean to them. It would be scary and embarrassing if she were, so I always went to play at their houses where it felt safer.

I didn't have much fun at the party. Mom didn't plan any games or activities, but the chocolate cake was my favorite, and I liked opening my presents. I felt happier when I shared them with my friends and we played together.

During my seventy-fourth year I attended a School of Womanly Arts event with more than two hundred women in Miami Beach. The purpose was to create fun and pleasure. That required looking within to contact our desires. We told each other about what we wanted, wrote our desires in the sand, and watched the ocean wash them away. We helped each other to claim them, visualize them, voice them, and make them detailed and specific. I could see us all becoming increasingly radiant as our desires felt more real. It reminded me of the happiness of my camp days and being part of a large, bonded group of friends again.

My biggest desire was to have a fabulous seventy-fifth birthday party that was over-the-top fun. I wanted a dazzling, elegant party where I felt beautiful, fully seen, and celebrated. A dear friend stepped up immediately and said she would make that happen. Without delay, she began to explore places in New York City that would meet my tastes and sensibilities. She called on my husband for his input on sites and menus, called on women in the group to help implement creative ideas for décor and entertainment, and asked me for a list of invitees. Her preparations went on for three months, attending to every detail with devotion and passion. I knew nothing about it but the name of the restaurant.

On the day of the party, I went to another friend's salon, where we played and giggled as she placed a glittering sunburst of diamond-like pins in my hair. I wore a one-shoulder golden dress adorned with sparkling sequins and felt like a light, twinkling and shimmering.

My Sister Goddess friends and my husband created a gorgeous party in a private room of a lavish New York City restaurant. There were luxurious carpets, richly colored plush chairs, sparkling chandeliers, bold paintings, and tables with tall candelabras and glistening crystal, strewn with red rose petals. It was my Diamond Birthday celebration!

Fifty excited friends of varying ages, all significantly younger than I, overflowed with happiness. My devoted husband gave an eloquent toast of love, evoking feelings of fulfillment or longings in every woman in the room. I wished they could all feel so treasured. We did a sexy tango, so at one with each other that several told me they were mesmerized by our connection. Dressed as goddesses with diamonds real and faux, many offered warm, touching toasts. Bouquets of compliments were sprinkled throughout an evening filled with happy recollections, gratitude, laughter, laughter, and more laughter! The room was filled with a play-list of music I adore, prepared by another friend.

One friend sang my favorite song "Imagine." Others did an adorable, cheeky dance draped in pink boas. Another wrote and performed a witty original lyric to "Mame" titled "Jane" that was heartwarming, brilliant, and funny. It touched me to my core and brought me to my feet, jumping up and down with glee! It was a moment of exuberant joy that I will never forget. My eyes were fixed on the stage, yet once I turned to embrace the group I saw all the women standing around the perimeter of the room swaying to the music, waving their arms overhead in rhythm, and singing yet another chorus of "Jane." We all squealed with delight—and did an encore!

Your fierce desire moves through us all, Jane.

And motivates us when we feel stalled, Jane.

You came to Mama Gena's and absolutely nothing is the same.

You're special fascination'll—prove to be inspirational

We think you're just sensational Jane, Jane, Jane, Jane

JANE!!!!!

That was the most thrilling night of my life. My five-year-old and seventy-five-year-old selves both showed up at my birthday party feeling known and loved, having more fun than I can ever remember. This was the big, happy family I had always wished for, a family in which I belonged.

More than anything, my five-year-old self had wanted attention, to be known, recognized, and adored. I wanted to be the kind of light that reflected in my mother's face when I walked into the room from something I said or did that pleased her or simply from the pride and pleasure of my presence. That never happened. Yet the glorious outpouring of love I received from these sisters on that night filled my unmet longing, as it still does to this day.

When I got home I was so excited that I couldn't sleep. I sat by myself for a long time, digesting the evening. I had come so far from the suffocating invisibility I suffered in my childhood home and had felt most painfully at Walt's Bar Mitzvah. I thought about how that happened, how I got from there to here.

Passionate attention to my inner journey brought me from my "good girl" role to my soul. Decades spent unraveling my history, letting go of my false self-image and the choices that supported it while prioritizing pleasure delivered me to my own radiance. My seventy-fifth birthday party was a victory lap, a reward for my years of introspection. My self-love was mirrored back to me fifty-fold. Thrilled by that realization, I went to sleep humbled and ecstatic.

thirty five

BOB'S VICTORY

BOB WAS BECOMING MORE OPEN TO HIMSELF AND MORE transparent with me. Our years of conversation about beliefs, emotions, and spirituality had taken hold. He wanted to understand himself and to spend time with people and activities that pleased him. He wanted to return to the happiness he felt when we came together. Gradually what he produced mattered less to him and how he was feeling and being mattered more. He was blossoming before my eyes!

We were both retired from our long-standing careers. I made that adjustment happily, but Bob found it difficult. When I ended my counseling practice, Bob was envious of how easily and gracefully I did so. I enjoyed the freedom to fill my hours as I pleased. He knew that I delighted in my work, but he also saw that my self-worth was not tied to it. It was not my identity.

Bob wanted that freedom for himself. His greatest challenge was letting go of his self-definition as a business leader, especially since he no longer was one. What he thought had given him value was not available. He didn't feel powerful and productive.

Not knowing what else to do, he finally accepted my suggestion to begin journal writing, looking inside for his answers.

Immediately Bob saw that he had always focused on his strengths of intellect and success, while avoiding areas where he felt less able: relationships and intimacy. Exploring himself emotionally required his willingness to shift from being a knower and doer to being a learner. He was frequently uncomfortable, feeling frustrated, lacking and lost, but he persevered.

Bob judged his vulnerabilities harshly. He knew I was aware of them and was amazed that I accepted them. I reminded him that we are all works in progress. He entertained the possibility that, since I could accept all of him, maybe he could too. Perhaps he could give himself that kindness.

Strengthened by my years with Mama Gena and the Sister Goddess community, I was able to take the lead in our relationship. By receiving community support, I was less subject to Bob's struggle. I was grateful for his strengths and his willingness to look into himself. I kept myself happy most of the time and continued to plan pleasurable activities. When Bob was mired in old behaviors, I gently reminded him to check inside while I took some space.

Bob began to look for interests that he would enjoy on his own. Returning to a fond memory from his Yale days, he joined a men's *a cappella* chorus, looking forward to his weekly singing rehearsals. He even had the thrill of singing with his chorus at Carnegie Hall! Bob also became a mentor, counseling and giving marketing workshops, helping clients to start or expand their professional dreams. He spent time with our children and played with our grandchildren. Most of all, he put his attention on our relationship, finding it the richest and most rewarding part of his life.

As stubborn as Bob can be, I felt him melting with my touch and devotion. My softness continued to thaw his internal barriers, and he began to open to his vulnerabilities. Little by little he started to accept them as part of himself, a magic step toward intimacy. How much easier it was for me to connect with his true vulnerability than to be frozen out by a veneer of false confidence and strength.

I happily received Bob's attention, which encouraged him to give more. I continued to play with him, flirt with him, and laugh with him, and he was delightfully responsive. Feeling internally stronger, he became more loving and transparent. He saw that expressing his vulnerabilities increased our emotional intimacy and sexual connection. He realized that people who express vulnerabilities are easier to love than those who hide them.

Although still intermittently caught in fear and pain, Bob was increasingly in touch with his big heart. He was grateful for my daily presence, love, receptivity, and enthusiasm. It delighted him to be the mirror I dreamed of all my life, consistently offering acknowledgements I never heard from my parents or first husband. I believe he wanted to make up for my difficult years before him and with him. I felt loved as never before.

Bob's victory was my victory too. My inner journey inspired him to reach for his own. Soul selfishness had given me much happiness and he wanted that for himself. We both came to see that self-love, the gift of connecting to our souls, is the foundation of all satisfying, happy relationships.

Recently, we boarded a plane to return home. We were sitting in the first row. As the plane took off, our flight attendant, Michelle, was about a yard away, facing us from her folding seat. She was an attractive woman, about forty, outgoing with a ready smile. Bob was reading to me. He enjoys that and I love it when he does. Both of us were deeply into an emotionally involving story. I was leaning over the partition separating us to hear more easily as the engines revved.

After landing, while taxiing to our gate, Michelle told us that she was watching us as Bob read. She said to me, "That was the sweetest thing I ever saw, until I looked at your face looking at Bob. That was even sweeter than the sweetest thing I ever saw."

She continued, "You two are like high school lovers. Dear God, I wish all of us could be loved like that."

thirty six

MORTALITY

WHILE I WAS IN ARIZONA, ONE OF MY FRIENDS SUGGESTED
that I would find it interesting and expansive to attend the service of an acclaimed faith healer. Eight years later, I went to
The Little Chapel for the first time. How fortunate it was that I
went and experienced Sara O'Meara, days before my frightening
bleeding episode.

Sara lives on a beautiful estate at the base of Camelback
Mountain in Paradise Valley. She holds monthly services there.
Many years earlier Sara had been healed of advanced cancer by
another faith healer, Kathryn Kuhlman, and was told it was her
work to do that for others. She has been graciously serving in
this way for three decades. During that time, thousands of people
attending the services have been miraculously healed, many from
incurable or what seemed like impossible conditions. I was glad
to be there as it felt so sacred and tranquil. Listening to testimonials of others' healings was beyond my comprehension, yet
I actually saw miracles happen.

A few days after attending the service, I was terrified to look into the toilet and see blood—never a good sign at age seventy-eight. A moment of panic overtook me. My Dad's first sign of prostate cancer was bloody urine. My husband's first sign of kidney cancer was the same. Alarmed, I wondered, "Do I have cancer?"

I was far away from my trusted gynecologist in New York. After long distance conversations and visits with a local doctor, I decided to follow their independent, identical opinions that it was prudent to have a full hysterectomy. My immediate thought: "Oh no, not my uterus. That is the place that held my four babies. They were a part of me as I was a part of them. We were joined physically, energetically, and spiritually." Tears welled up as I remembered my pregnancies, feeling the first signs of new life inside me. I will never forget those faint, delicate fluttering sensations. Later on, tiny feet or elbows pushed outward, creating odd shapes in my swollen belly. I remembered my tender feelings when the increased movements kept me up at night as the babies grew toward term. Then I reminded myself, "Jane, that was a very long time ago."

For many years, my daily focus had changed dramatically from mothering to my professional life. I have and always will give time, attention, and love to my family, yet they have happily and successfully established their own lives—marriages, families, careers, homes, friendships, and interests. They are doing well on their own.

The impending surgery made real to me how long it had been since my children had thrived within me. I realized that I was now in a late stage of my life, and I began to think about death. I realized that if I am to live the next years fully, it is necessary to accept my death as an intrinsic part of my life.

What if this condition turns out to be invasive cancer? What do I do if the doctors inform me that chemotherapy and radiation are needed to stem the cancerous growth? I could feel myself getting increasingly tense, my stomach in knots, and my eyes wanting to close. I couldn't accept that it is necessary to destroy healthy cells to kill unhealthy ones, nor to do what makes me sick so that I can be well. Soon after being told that I needed surgery I called Sara, who promised to pray for me, which was a comfort, even though I felt I was grasping for straws. While I wanted to believe, I was skeptical. She told me that all would be well.

How deep is my faith? What trust do I give to Sara who has received a faith healing and has facilitated healing for thousands? How much am I willing to trust witnessing healings that happened right before my eyes and testimonials from people who had experienced dramatic healings and were changed forever? I went to sleep after listening to an audiotape, reminding myself that every cell in my body has its own intelligence and knows how to heal itself. The next morning I woke up with comforting thoughts. Often my first thoughts seem to be very pure. "Never do what you don't want to do. What is good for others may not be good for you. Do not go against yourself or judge others. Ever. Go your own way."

I thought, "I don't know how many days I have left on this planet. I want my days here to be peaceful ones and my decisions to be compatible with what I believe." I was convinced that regardless of the diagnosis I would not undergo chemotherapy. I would make my life the happiest it could be, every day I was here. If necessary I would travel the world to find a process that I trusted as effective. That would be a far happier journey. A feeling of peace came over me, and I was able to rest.

As the day of surgery approached I was relieved to get on with it, yet anxious about what the surgeon would find. While I had full confidence in him, I was greatly concerned about what was happening in my uterus. The hospital was new, bright, and comfortable, and the nurses were well trained and compassionate. Bob was with me until the last moment, and I welled up as we said goodbye.

He was at my bedside when I awoke after surgery and I immediately asked, "What did he find?"

"He found a small cancer in your uterus, Jane, and since it was close to a lymph portal, he took eight nodes for biopsy in addition to the organs he removed. He thinks it's OK, but felt it prudent to do that."

"Cancer. Lymph nodes. This is a big deal. A shocking big deal!"

"Don't worry, honey," Bob said. "It's probably OK." I could feel the emptiness in his words as I looked into his eyes, where I saw deep sadness.

The next morning the surgeon arrived and began to quickly repeat what Bob had told me. Rather than request that he slow down, I asked him to please draw a picture of what he saw and what he did. I knew a visual would be easier for me to comprehend. I looked at his drawings several times that day, trying to get a handle on what had happened. The drawing showed the small cancerous mass alarmingly close to the lymphatic portal. It was hard to believe that I could be dealing with systemic cancer after major surgery, when just a few days earlier I had been walking on a treadmill at four miles an hour.

The doctor also said that the results would probably not be back for five or six days due to the weekend, and that he doesn't discuss test results on the phone. He scheduled my follow-up appointment eleven days later. I didn't fully grasp how that would feel, but waiting that long seemed endless.

I was scared, really scared, consciously facing mortality for the first time. All that I had read and thought I believed about how idyllic life after death would be evaporated. Was this my time? For years I had read books and studied about death. I read there was only physical death and that our souls go on, that death is a peaceful release, the ultimate letting go. I heard that we go to a far more beautiful place, and when returning to "the other side" we see our loved ones who have passed before us.

So why was I scared? Why was my mind and body terrified every moment except when I was writing, focusing on more creative thoughts? If I fully believed that death would be a heavenly transition, I would not have these uncomfortable physical responses: a tight belly, headaches, and no appetite.

I saw that I didn't really trust all the beautiful things I'd read and heard about death. Instead I thought: How long will I be here? How many days are left to me? How shall I spend them? Where and with whom?

My mind raced on: "How much will I suffer? Will I have pain? Will it be bearable? What will happen to Bob? Will I have the grace to encourage him to find another love when I am gone? What has my life been about? What do I want to complete? Where do I want my belongings to be placed? What songs do I want at my funeral? Will I suffer? That thought keeps coming back. Will I suffer? Will I have a painful or peaceful death? Is it possible that in the end there is nothing? Will I just be ashes in an urn?"

I didn't want to believe that, yet my body was telling me how scared I was. "Why am I kidding myself? All I see is a void. Maybe I will be surprised."

The best remedy I had in those days of waiting was writing, since the mind can focus on only one thing at a time. It was a godsend indeed. I answered well-wishers' texts and emails, but not phone calls other than from our children. It was a time where children came forth to nurture mother.

I allowed myself to rest in Bob's love, which was profoundly consoling. I didn't want to leave his side. Just holding his hand gave me peace. We sat in the comfortable shade at the community club, I writing my stories and he editing them. We prepared meals together, read together, watched TV together, cuddled together, and napped together. I slept a lot, and well. Sweet sleep was such a reprieve. No thoughts, just rest.

Late on the fifth day after surgery, I received a call from the surgeon. I knew it was good news because he'd said he wouldn't discuss test results on the phone. He told me that all lymph nodes came back clean, that the cancer in my uterus was tiny and that it had only minimally invaded the uterine wall. No further treatment would be necessary, only five years of observation. It was the best possible result! I thanked him profusely for the good news call that saved Bob and me six more days of anxiety.

I felt great relief immediately, fully accepting the report. To celebrate, I asked Bob if he wanted to tango but he apologized, saying he wasn't up for that. All the fears he had repressed to get through these days, all the pain and past memories of his own and other family members' cancer surgeries overtook him. He needed time alone. It was now my opportunity to comfort him.

Bob and I went to The Little Chapel for a service a few days later. When I told Sara the good news she was pleased but not surprised. Soon after Sara called the congregation to prayer, I felt a cool fluttering feeling over my upturned palms. In my mind's eye I saw large white feathers gently flapping. The feeling increased as the feathers multiplied and the gentle movement cooled my face, neck, and heart. It was the sweetest, softest, most beautiful feeling. Then it stopped. I believed that I had been touched by Spirit. Feelings rose from my belly upward to my eyes as soft, warm tears trickled down my cheeks. I was moved in a way unknown to me, filled with peace, pure peace.

For several days I experienced deep emotional releases. I became more present to the gift of life, to its beauty and its suffering. Realizing that the only time I have is now, I asked myself: "Am I using my energy primarily in behalf of my true desires or am I abdicating to others, their perceived needs and wants? These had become my ongoing soul selfish questions.

When I went for my post-surgery check-up, the doctor told me that while he has done more than a thousand such procedures, mine was unique. He said that it is most unusual for a pathologist to bring a preliminary report into the operating room, suggesting further surgery. If he had concluded the surgery before that input, I would have had to undergo another operation with all the emotional concern and physical discomfort accompanying it. I believe that was Divine intervention.

When I was well enough to travel it was time to return to my home back East. Sitting in the airplane, I was filled with gratitude. I had spent a gorgeous winter with my husband in Arizona, culminating in a life-saving hysterectomy and spiritual awakening. Now, many times a day, I remind myself of what I learned in The Little Chapel. "I am God's treasured creation." I remind myself that you are, too.

thirty seven

PARIS

I WAS ONE OF A GROUP OF SEVENTY WOMEN FROM THE School of Womanly Arts who went to Paris to take in and enjoy the beauty it offers. Be it fashion, food, flowers, art, architecture, or simply the way the city was planned, the feminine value for beauty abounds there.

I had been to Paris twice before, yet being with women friends is a different experience from traveling with husbands or children. We navigated the city in groups of four to seven, exploring the Metro and various neighborhoods. We walked through the Tuileries, where I was transfixed with Rodin's magnificent, almost lifelike statue *The Kiss*. We frequented bistros, browsed lingerie and designer shops, and followed the daily activities and destinations planned for us.

One morning five of us went to the park adjacent to the Palais Royal. We found some rickety chairs, made a circle and, one at a time, spent a long while telling the ways we appreciate each other. When it was my turn, I reclined in the middle of the circle and took some deep breaths to open myself to receive the appreciation about to be directed to me. It is strange that as much as I always longed for recognition, it did not feel natural or easy to accept. As I listened to their soul-filling impressions, I felt myself relax and enjoy it to the point where I laughed and said, "More, please!" Some compliments were familiar, warm and loving. Others were new and surprising, requiring more deep breaths. "You are strong in your soft and gentle manner, willing to be crazily unreasonable and live in the now, playful, fun-loving, ageless, the most enticing woman leading your man to his greatness." I felt that I was being bathed in love. To this day I return to these words when I feel low.

When we finished sharing acknowledgements and looked up, we noticed that there were many people standing back watching us. While clearly they did not know what we were doing or hear what we were saying, the uplifting energy that we transmitted must have traveled across the park.

Another highlight of Paris was going to visit the Palais Garnier opera house. It is a magnificent building, plush and grand with velvet seats and marble statues, fireplaces, wide hallways, and outdoor balconies. After exploring the grand interior, two of us were drawn to the music coming from outside and went onto a nearby balcony. There, in front of the opera house, was a huge crowd of people filling the steps, standing on the sides of the entrance, and draped over the statues. A steady stream of skilled performers played their instruments and sang songs, many that were American, which delighted the Parisians. It was a picture perfect day. As the two of us stood on our intricately carved balcony looking out at the people, listening to familiar music, seeing the pedestrians crossing the streets peacefully going about their business, we looked at each other filled to the brim with gratitude, gave each other a high-five and teared up as I said, "Can you believe this is our life?"

Toward the end of the trip I was asked to be in a movie

showing some of the high points of our time in Paris. How exciting, my first movie shoot! A little bit nervous, but excited, I woke up on Sunday morning, looked outside, and saw dark, heavy clouds. My heart sank. The movie shoot might be canceled, and the closing picnic could be spoiled. We were all asked to bring food and a small object we bought in Paris, which I planned to buy at the outdoor market. I got dressed and went downstairs for breakfast, feeling concerned and disappointed about the weather, hoping for a glorious, warm, sunny day. Meeting my friends in the dining room immediately perked me up, and those of us in the shoot were ready for whatever the plan might be.

The van picked us up on time and brought us a few feet away to the Champs-Elysee. We were filmed walking in clusters of two and three with our open umbrellas, ending with a posed shot closing and then leaning on them. We were then scheduled to go to an outdoor market, but since it was pouring, we went to a landmark patisserie instead. It seemed like we were there forever tasting all kinds of beautiful pastries, croissants, and bonbons while being filmed. Delectable. French butter definitely makes pastries taste divine! Feeling full and happy, we moved on to the Eiffel Tower. Seeing the Tower in its entirety from close range was breathtaking.

Each of us was filmed individually as well as with the group. Standing on a platform, we were asked to physically express our feelings about Paris. I did that with a big smile and open arms, seductively closing them to embrace myself as well as the City of Light. Others blew kisses, danced, and some curtsied to the Tower. Such fun! The rain started again so we went to an outdoor café and sat around several small tables pulled together under a canopy waiting for news about the picnic. We were served café, cappuccino, tea, and several platters of rolls and pastries. We were having the best time, unconcerned about the picnic while the rain continued to stream down from the canopy.

Eventually word came that they found a small tent structure in the Tuileries that made the event possible. When we arrived we saw tables already filled with cheeses, fruits, breads and rolls, canapés, charcuterie, pastries, and a huge bucket of ice filed with champagne bottles. Even with so many of us there it didn't feel uncomfortable, rather more intimate than had we been spread out in the park as planned. We all felt physically, emotionally, and spiritually close and connected.

After a while the clouds parted and the sun came out. Interestingly, most of the women remained in the tent huddled together. Since I was yearning for warmth and sunshine, I walked onto the grass toward a wide walking path. Feeling grateful and at one with myself, my friends and this beautiful place, I lifted my arms to the heavens and began to dance. Completely unselfconscious, I danced with a level of joy and freedom new to me, filled with community connection, the fun of the movie shoot, the intimacy and abundance of the picnic, and the warmth of the sun. I was overflowing, feeling the beauty of Paris, myself, and the life I was living.

When I finally stopped, two women approached me. They were very simple women, wearing colorful crocheted caps, baggy clothes, and no make-up. They had been watching me and asked, "Are you an actress?" I answered that I was not. "A ballerina? You are so graceful, the way you carry your body, your shoulders, and your head. The way you move."

I thanked them for the compliments that meant more to me than they could ever have imagined. The ten-year-old girl living inside of me, wanting so much to be a Rockette had shown up. Yes, in my heart I am still a dancer! I began to chat with them and learned that they were from Russia. One had just lost her husband, and her sister thought it would be healing for them to take a trip to Paris together. We chatted for a while. I invited them to New York, and when it was time to part we stood together as sisters in a tender three-way hug.

I will never forget that day. I began it feeling heavy-hearted, thinking the rain might ruin the plans, and instead I learned I could make the day even better than I ever expected.

When it was time to end the picnic, each of us took a glass of champagne and Mama Gena gave a funny and passionate toast filled with her joy and appreciation for the trip, and for all of us coming. She had taken a big risk with this adventure and was thrilled that it turned out to be the delight she had envisioned. She ended her toast with: "Nothing outside of a woman can ever stop her from going for her pleasure."

I remember Mama Gena's words every day. They resonate through me, carrying within them every step of my soul selfish journey, what I now realize is my own unstoppable pursuit of my happiness. I have learned to find the jewels in both my "good" and my "bad" circumstances. I have learned to accept love and appreciation as easily as I give it. I have learned to forgive, to let go, to trust my heart and my mind, to speak up for myself the way no "good girl" ever could.

Am I being selfish these days? Some might say that I am. Listening to my soul gives me a rest from the busyness of my ego-driven mind desiring to prove itself, feel worthy, and be loved. I have stood for my solitude, despite the judgments of people who don't understand or share that desire. As I connect more to my soul, I look less to others for approval and direction.

I feel the preciousness of my life. No more time to waste. No more "doing the right thing," putting up with undesirable behavior from others, or putting off what is important to me. I believe our souls are connected, that it is only our egos that separate us. The more I make soul choices, the more I happily accept that I have become soul selfish for my sake and ultimately for the sake of those lives I touch. I have more love to give. My journey is not for me alone.

epilogue

SOLO

Dreams of marriage: a loving, intimate, sexual, adventuresome and creative partnership. Yes, many a time it is all of that.

Dreams of family: unity, loyalty, celebration, friendship and fun. Yes, frequently. Yet my children and grandchildren live near and far away, and we are hardly ever all together. And they have their own dreams.

Beloved friends that I treasure, yet not forever. Lives and venues change. Closeness is elastic. Death comes, yet I cherish those who touch my soul, regardless of time and space.

Teachers, who have taught me how to live, to love and to be aware of my blessed life, have an abiding home forever in my mind and heart.

My Guides, who meet me daily in my stillness, tenderly supporting me where I am, or challenging me to take my next steps, continually bolstering my faith.

I sit here writing totally alone and happy to be. For I see that I, together with the Universe, am the only constant in my life, now with more willingness and time to settle in and listen.

So, self, what do you have to say?

I like being home. Even with winters, cold, gloomy, icy and windy as they can be, I like being home. I like my home, perched on a hill at the end of a long gravel driveway. Unpretentious and welcoming, each room in harmony with the whole. It is beautiful and always a comfort to me.

I like the short days and the darkness when the house is warm, and delicious smells of cooking food waft from the kitchen: fried onions, soups, poultry roasting. I like music filling the house, soft and gentle or loud and rocking. I like walking on my treadmill. I like fires crackling in the den while my husband reads to me. I like my books. I like learning. I like snuggling in bed under my feathery down quilt. I like making love. I like being home.

I like going to the Arizona desert: the dry air, the vast, cloudless, blue skies, the bright sunshine and clear light. I like the warmth on my body and the brightness defining each form. I like the stately saguaros, raising their arms to the heavens, the varied cacti, the distinctive smell of creosote after the rain. I like the mountains and the rocks, Native American spirituality and art. I like the soft energy, the quiet, the slower pace of life. I like the ease, spaciousness and freedom I feel there.

I like coming home, visiting with family. I like their warm welcomes and our celebration dinners. Catching up. Reconnecting. Going deeper than is possible from long distance. I like petting their dogs. I like playing with my grandkids and going on outings with them, singing in the car. I like when they sit on my lap and give me precious hugs.

I like going to New York City. I like being with my friends and spiritual community, the electricity of Broadway, especially the music and dancing. I like going to divine restaurants, watching skaters at Rockefeller Center, taking in the exquisite shop windows and light shows at Christmas.

I like doing my closets, changing them from season to season, taking stock of what I have and what I need. I like getting dressed up and feeling glamorous: chic outfits and chic venues. I like dancing.

I like traveling to foreign lands, the adventure of new sights, some that I have seen in photos, now real before my eyes. I like meeting and observing people so different in their customs, languages, style and food. I like that each country's personality is specifically its own. I like making new friends.

I like coming home. I like my car and driving through gorgeous country estates in Connecticut. I like the seasons—the bare trees weathering the storm, sometimes covered with crystals of ice, shimmering in the sun. I like the spring, with crocus, tulips and daffodils sprouting in early May. I like sitting on my screened porch. I like watching tiny leaves forming on tree branches, each day a little bigger until they open wide in a delicate shade of chartreuse. I like watching them mature into a deep green. I like my garden. I like my walks.

I like my life. I like myself. Simple words that have taken so long to utter and feel so sweet to say.

Dear reader, I wish you the same.

HOW SOUL SELFISH ARE YOU?

THE FOLLOWING QUESTIONS WILL GIVE YOU AN AWARENESS of where you are regarding soul selfishness at this moment in time. The quiz will offer you a fuller understanding of what being soul selfish means, and provide you with a map for future growth.

Score yourself on a scale of 0 – 5, with 5 being fully satisfied:

How much do you prioritize you pleasure?   _____

How aware are you of your desires?   _____

How much energy do you put out to fulfill them?   _____

What priority do you give to alone time, listening to your inner self?

A. How aware are you of your emotional feelings?   _____

B. How much time do you give to journaling, meditation or prayer? _____

How self-caring are you?

A. Beauty _____

B. Health _____

C. Diet and physical fitness _____

D. Wardrobe _____

E. Leisure / Play _____

How easily do you receive:

A. Compliments _____

B. Gifts _____

C. Assistance _____

D. Emotional support _____

How able are you to say "No?" _____

How authentic is your "Yes?" _____

How satisfied are you with your closest relationship? _____

How connected are you to your friends? _____

How reliable is your support system? _____

How self-forgiving are you? _____

How forgiving of others are you? _____

How willing are you to spend money on yourself? _____

How much do you laugh? _____

TOTAL SCORE: _____

In order to reach your destination you need to know where you are. Your score is simply your starting point on your way to becoming more self-loving—more soul-selfish!

0 – 25   This range ranks you as a novice, with great opportunity to grow.

26 – 50   This range puts you firmly on the path to becoming soul selfish, and offers much chance to improve.

51 – 75   This range means you are well on your way—and with every intention of going higher.

76 – 100 This range means you are far along on your path—Congratulations!

Over 100 WOW, you have really learned what it means to be soul selfish. What a great model you are for others!

ABOUT THE AUTHOR

IN HER MEMOIR *Soul-Selfish: The Awakening of a "Good Girl,"* Jane Wyker shares the vast experience of her forty-six-year inner journey. Working in over a dozen different psychological, mind-body, and spiritual disciplines, she had the courage and faith to follow the guidance of many teachers and, ultimately, her own soul. Now eighty, she models a life that is created from within, demonstrating that sustained happiness rests upon soul connection. She is still learning.

A graduate of Cornell University and a former elementary school teacher, Jane was a pioneer in parent education. She opened her Parents School before "parenting" was a word and created communities for mothers to share and support each other with new child-rearing concepts. Participants in her school soon requested private sessions, leading to the start of her twenty-nine-year Family Counseling practice. Jane worked with individuals, couples, and groups dealing with self-development, marriage, parenting, career, and loss. She later turned her focus to presenting seminars for men and women in Fortune

500 companies, helping them to balance their work and family lives. It was a topic she understood intimately as she managed her thriving career while raising her four children and pursuing her own spiritual growth.

Jane's journey has taken her through marriage, parenting, divorce, forgiveness, loss, and new love. She has traveled the world, dancing the tango in Argentina, playing with her friends in Paris, observing the elderly practice Tai Chi in Hong Kong, and exploring the awesome sights of ancient Egypt. She has similarly navigated her inner world, continually examining her beliefs, releasing long-held pain, and forging an intimate and trusting relationship with her true self. She learned that when she is selfish enough to take care of her soul connection, love and wisdom flow. She believes that is true for all of us.